The Toroidal Zodiac

Beyond the Wheel

Tess Hadley Durand

For Geo, a *most* spirited nature!

Introduction

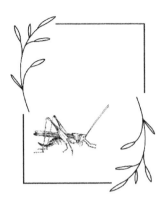

When you think of nature, what comes to your mind? Take a moment and think about it. Maybe you hear birds singing or trees blowing in the breeze. Maybe you see light sparkling along a river, ice on the mountains, fish in the sea, tigers charging across the Sahara or caterpillars inching along a bright green leaf. Maybe you feel the crispness of autumn air, the hot sand beneath your feet, the pelting rain or the crunch of snow.

Now think about the fact that all of this activity is happening now, all around the world. The immense amount of activity is impossible to measure. In any frame of nature at any point in time, activity is bustling. It may be overt as a flock of seagulls diving for fish or as unassuming as a seemingly empty field of grass. But a closer look at the field reveals a teaming of activity. The insects are bustling, the seeds are sprouting, the elements and nutrients are dancing about in their chemical exchanges. The bustle of activity is the serenity of nature. The Earth that never sleeps is a peaceful blue green sphere.

Compare the gentle chirping of one cricket outside your window to the wash of hundreds of crickets chirping in a meadow. The wash of activity is the serenity of nature. Nature is not the business of half-hearted pursuits. It is the height of bustling activity. The interrelated bustle is nature's peace. A waterfall crashes down upon rocks. Its immeasurable power is its deep peace. Its magnitude is its health.

A bee collects nectar from a sun soaked flower. Its purpose and competence is its joy. Activity is happily married to a sense of purpose. You simply don't see a woodpecker taking no interest in trees. The light of spirit is too bright to go unrecognized. A dolphin leaping out from the sea is a triumph, a celebration. A little proud bird on top of a pine tree is an anthem of self belief, backed by the power of nature and its bustle of activity.

Spiritedness is without limit. Deep peace is without limit. These things are one and the same. In the heights of joyous activity and movement come the deepest feelings of peace. The wash of a cricket meadow is the electricity within you. You only need to tune in.

This book was written to help you tune in.

Two Kinds of Time

Time is a game played beautifully by children. Heraclitus

My World is a children's book by Margaret Wise Brown. My son and I read this at night under a cactus light. The opening page shows a mother reading to her child by a fire. The words are "The fire burns. The pages turn".[1]

I started thinking about the nature of time. Some time seems to turn but some time seems to burn. Some time comes back around and some time trailblazes the future and celebrates the spirit. These two kinds of time blend together yet they are inherently different. One is bound to law and one is free. One is used to gain more control and one is embraced to live as lively as possible. One is a clock and one is a flower. One is a wheel. What is the shape of the other? What is the shape of the spirited time that burns like the sun and illuminates meaning in the lives we live?

The wheel of the zodiac turns. Its twelve archetypes carry the meaning of the seasons that turn. The meaning of the seasons is so charged that it goes beyond the snow and heat. It extends into the mystery of the seasons of life, and all the relations of living. The wheel turns and time folds in on itself. This summer compares to last summer. The winter is prepared for because we know it is coming. What emerges from this turning is the potential for more and more meaning. The wheel has the capacity to become a generator; a maker of more knowledge and light. The pages turn but the fire burns.

I began to think about the experiential side of time. Some time is "heights" and some time is "depths". Some time is more middle ground.

The heights of time are the joys, the unbridled laughter, the perfection of a day. This time rushes over the body like a shower of effervescence. This time is *lived.* It isn't turning on an abstract clock, *you* are turning; towards the light, like a daisy or an actor on the stage. This time burns bright in the heights of one's heart.

"Depth" time carries a force of memory and a sense of belonging. Depth time can anchor you "home" or polarize you to "true north". It can also sink you with despair. Depth time carries the echoes of your ancestors and the aromas of your most desired dreams. Its gravity is undeniably in the body.

"Middle ground" time is for managing the business of living. Our bodies are blessed with the genius of nervous systems. All of the information and interaction that we encounter gets integrated into the "system" of the body. Biofeedback has evolved for centuries. Our systems are cutting edge. Middle ground time embraces the coolness of logic, the sureness of morality, and the feedback of physicality.

My new question was: if time is a wheel that turns, how does this other time move? Is there any order to it? My instinct said yes.

Time and Turning

To everything (turn, turn, turn) Pete Seeger

If you were to sit in one spot and look out a window for your entire life you would still see the seasons change. You would witness the leaves turn the sunset hues of fall. You would behold winter turning into spring and spring turning into summer. Even if you never turned your head, the seasons would continue turning. But would you have turned into the person you are today?

Turning is analogous to time. A flower turns each day to the light. The earth turns. Day turns to night and back to day. The map of stars turns. The pages of the calendar turn as do the hands on the clock. *And we turn.* We turn bigger. We turn older. But our turning doesn't cycle back like the turning of clocks and calendars. Our turning goes onward. We have the capacity to turn into wiser, kinder, more able people. We have the capacity to turn into the person we want to become. We have the capacity to turn mundane time into special and meaningful time.

Though the seasons continue to turn whether you witness them or not, there is no divorcing the time that you *do* witness from yourself. You *are* that time. When you come back from a weekend trip people ask, how was your time? It is a question of your experience; of you with your world at that time.

The zodiac wheel turns and allows us to look at the relationships within cyclic time. It allows us to integrate our understanding of how time moves in order to make the most of time.

But there is another shape to consider when it comes to the actual time that is *experienced.* To experience time means to live that time in the here and no within all of the ebbs and flows of history, environment, body and circumstance. The shape that can best embody this complexity is the torus field: a self-regulating shape that is found everywhere in nature.

A torus is the shape of a donut, but the hole in the center can be infinitely small. Two vortexes on each end run through a central axis. It draws the wider part back through one vortex, into the middle and back out the other vortex where it snakes around to do it again, continuously. This is the movement of a tornado or a whirlpool. This is the movement of an energy field.

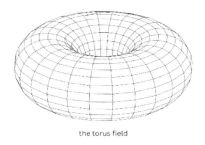

the torus field

The torus field flows. It flows like the time you might experience on holidays or in a place of deep focus. It flows like our breath. It has the capacity to flow smoother and stronger or weaker and more erratic. The wheel is based on law but the torus is based on freedom. The torus introduces a most natural element of spontaneity that the wheel has no use for. If the wheel was based on freedom then no one could ever be certain of leaving work at 3:00, or setting a wedding date for June 7th. Likewise if a torus field was based on law instead of freedom then a person's life would be completely pre-determined and they may as well sit by that window for all of their days.

The freedom within the torus fields transforms the wheel's 'continuous turning' into a *capacity to turn'* or *'choose'*. The word horoscope is derived from the Greek words *ōra* and *scopos* meaning "time" and "observer". *Toro* is Latin for "bull" but it also means "to steer". Turning thus becomes steering when the zodiac bases itself on freedom instead of law.

We are more like plants than we realize. Plants convert pure light into sustenance. It is the same light that falls upon the words you are reading now as well as the light that lights up your mind, your heart and your spirits. Just like the plant, we turn the light of meaning into sustenance, and we build our lives with this nourishment.

The more we can claim the act of 'turning' as our own the better we can understand time's metabolism. The better we can learn to navigate the time we live the more we can understand our true selves. We are the time that burns when *we turn,* when we steer our own ship. The more conscious the turning, the more vibrant the burning.

The circle of the zodiac is complete; a perfect 360 degrees. But our year has 365 days. Those extra 5 days, let alone leap year days (and leap seconds!) inform us of a sacred truth. Life is not a perfect round circle, it is still growing. Life aspires, it breathes. There is much to learn from cycles and circles. But we fundamentally are not circles and cycles, we are more like spirals and paths. Spirals are really circles in the act of growing. In fact, *the act of growing is what connects us to nature* and makes us one with it. In embracing our growth, our conscious turning, we become more natural, more connected to our powers which are based in nature.

Metabolism comes from the Greek word "metabole" which means 'change'. Cyclic time shows an inherent order to change, as do the beautiful golden ratio patterns on display in the natural world. The metabolism in the body demonstrates remarkable order as well with its complex biochemical processes firing away at all times.

But when it comes to change in your life, how much order is there to it? The places where change either leads to order or creates more order are likely places that you feel good about. To see the order that you created in your life from the seas of change that are inevitable is to stand beside your great work, and feel a sense of honor, or spirit. This is your true self; the part of you with the capacity to turn, the 'readiness' within that is capable of creating great works. You can move against the most fundamental law of nature which is the law of entropy. Order can be stored instead of lost. You can learn to keep absorbing and turning to more light.

Metabolism is defined as the chemical processes that occur within a living organism in order to maintain life. Mitochondria converting food to energy is one example, but so is a compliment that makes you feel good. Every passing moment has to do with chemical processes continually changing. We certainly need water and food for survival but after our basic survival needs are met there are other things to metabolize. There are things that feed a sense of well-being and other things that quench a thirst for discovery.

What are these things? What are these things for *you*? What fills you up? What fortifies you? Satisfies you? What do you hold on to? What allows you not merely to survive but thrive?

When it comes to the toroscope, time scales are not important. A moment, a year or a lifetime all show examples of 'things' that sustain us and fill us up. A memory of admiring a sea shell as a child on vacation might waft through the awareness of a marine biologist.

When my father was a boy he loved to listen to Mel Allen relay the yankee games on the radio. His father often told him to turn it off and get busy with something else. Until one day as an adult, he was hired by MLB productions to write *This Week in Baseball* for Mel Allen. His father loved the show and took it all back! He also got a kick out of telling his colleagues that he thought his son was wasting time when in fact he was planting seeds for a future.

A moment, a year or a lifetime, a special kind of engagement transcends it all. When you recognize a part of yourself in something else, there is magic at play. From a distance you may be able to put some pieces together and get a glimpse of your self-designed butterfly wing.

Throughout the chapters of this book, we will be moving through the toroscope. What was once Aries to Taurus to Gemini with the wheel becomes Taurus to Gemini to Virgo. It is a different order. It is not the order of the time that turns, it is the order of the time that illumines. The more we can understand this order, the better we can metabolize time and convert the light of meaning into true sustenance. We can learn the secrets of flow and being 'in the zone'. We can remember that 'normal' is really a state of readiness that embraces productive activity. We can see the merits of solitude and focus in a highly distracted world. There is no divorcing ourselves from nature. Our powers are the powers of nature. We are alienated from them insofar as we are alienated from nature. Nature grows with us and shares her creative powers.

The Toroscope

If we are to explore time in terms of heights and depths, we are going to need a new model. The wheel no longer serves the purpose. Up and down is measured vertically, so we will need a line. The top represents the apex of heights while the bottom represents the abyss of depths.

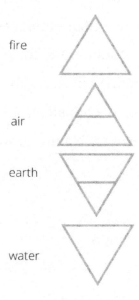

The zodiac consists of four elements. Each element contains three signs to make a triangle, a circuit of energy flow. The ancients expressed the elements in four triangles, with Fire and

Air pointing upward and Earth and Water pointing downward. A line runs through the triangles of Earth and Air to signify a limit. This is to say that while Air goes up, it does not go all the way up and while Earth goes down it does not go all the way down.

What does this mean?

Let's begin by considering a world without limits. What would happen if gravity no longer held you to the earth? How about if you went the rest of your life without another wink of sleep or abandoned all moral instinct? Limits are needed to keep life in balance. Homeostasis is hard at work. Physicality has its limits as does perception and thinking. Injury and moral issues reveal a bodily threshold that must be grappled with. The Earth element reveals a biologically-rooted morality which informs our logic as we ascend into the realm of Air with thought and thinking. Just as the air in our atmosphere is breathable only up to the stratosphere, intellect can only go so far in search of truth. Beyond thinking lies the eternal world of light, an unshakable vitality of fire. Beneath the earth of physicality and tangibility lies the ineffable quality of feelings; a water that runs all the way down.

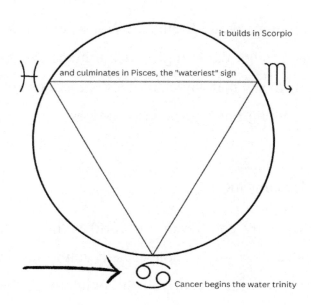

it builds in Scorpio

and culminates in Pisces, the "wateriest" sign

Cancer begins the water trinity

Deep in the abyss of the zodiac swim the fish. Pisces is the eternal dreamer, the ultimate yin. The water element begins with Cancer then builds into Scorpio and finally culminates in Pisces. This makes Pisces the accumulation of water, the *wateriest* water sign and it belongs at the bottom of our line. It is the poetic sublime and the everything of all. It is the wash of the cricket meadow; the deep peace of nature's interrelated activity.

♃	sagittarius	♐
☉	leo	♌
♂	aries	♈
♅	aquarius	♒
♀	libra	♎
☿	gemini	♊
♀	taurus	♉
☿	virgo	♍
♄	capricorn	♑
☽	cancer	♋
♇	scorpio	♏
♆	pisces	♓

Sagittarius, the apex of fire, celebrates the high times. It is pure spiritedness and freedom. The Archer's arrow leads all of evolution forward, with enthusiasm! From Aries, fire builds into Leo and at last culminates in Sagittarius as pure spiritedness.

To complete this new model we just need to fill in the rest of the signs. Earth culminates in Capricorn so it will be lower on the line, heavier and more dense. Air culminates in Aquarius so it will be higher, just before the burst of fire. The vertical line can be expressed by the signs or by the planets that rule these signs.

It's a good time to pause. We have a new map of the zodiac. The same signs are in a different order. It represents something different now. The wheel represented the turning of time. It tick-tocks like a clock. But the line doesn't do that. It goes up and down like the tides of our very existence.

What do we see in this new model? What new patterns? What new ideas come forth?

A pair of Mercuries caught my eye. They stood above and below Venus, the sign of Taurus, the sign of self-love. This brought to mind an eloquent definition of a consciousness I had recently heard. Neuroscientist Antonio Damasio defines a conscious mind as "a mind with a self in it".[2] I drew a circle around the Mercuries to make "mind".

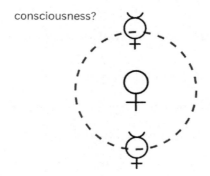

The glyph of Mercury is the same as the glyph of Taurus, just atop a cross. It is as if the self (Taurus) entered into a world of opposites, a world of East, West, North and South. A world of

Spring, Summer, Fall and Winter. And, like Alice through the looking glass, noticed that things became curious and curiouser.

The next circle I drew connected Venus and Saturn (Libra and Capricorn). I knew that Saturn naturally exalts in Venus' sign of Libra, but I wondered what it meant in terms of this emerging diagram. Then came a circle connecting the thunderbolt of Uranus to the soothing waters of the Moon (Aquarius and Cancer). I hadn't ever seen these planets paired before. How does the detached airs of awareness and genius pair with the private waters of inner life and family? The answer would prove to amaze me.

Another "natural" looking pair ensued with Mars (Aries) and Pluto who share common rule over the swirling waters of Scorpio. The next circle shows the Sun connecting to Neptune (Leo and Pisces). Dreamy Neptune exalts in the golden aurum of the Sun, so some logic followed this one too.

Then came a halt. Jupiter (Sagittarius) is without a partner. For a flash it seemed this was all without meaning. It was as if the idea of reordering the zodiac was like shuffling an ordered deck of cards into a mess. But then I noticed something important. I noticed that Taurus, ruled by Venus, was also without a partner. Though cozy in the middle of it all she had no one to dance with. I connected these two "wallflowers" to each other and stepped back again to see what was there.

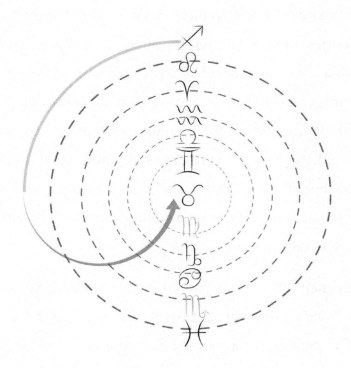

It became instantly clear to me. This was no longer a line but a rotating "field". This was an energy field. The deepest center draws from the farthest reach. It moves. It sustains itself with its movement. This is not ticking or tocking, it is breathing.

I was reminded of a book I had read by inventor and cosmologist Arthur M. Young called "The Reflexive Universe".

He writes that all living creatures in the universe are toroidal, or torus-shaped.

Young also believes the universe itself to be torus-shaped; a living, breathing field of energy of which we are intimately a part of as well as sharply distinct from.[3] All living creatures relate to their world "reflexively", that is to say in a way that refers back to themselves. We relate ourselves to what we experience and continue to radiate ourselves back out into experience. A simpler expression might be: experience shapes you so that you can shape experience. The torus shape is the shape that invites one to join in on the shaping. The true shape of nature is a god who invites its creations to be co-creators.

The future of the zodiac was always encoded in the wheel. For "future" stems from the latin root "fu" which means "to grow". Ordered vertically, the zodiac resembles a plant that grows. Its roots pull water from the depths as it faces and reaches for the light of sun in the heights.

For the plant and the animal, the future is not abstract. It is married to the body. *Future is the capacity to grow*, to become, to assert one's magnitude, relate wholeheartedly and go about one's "business." This kind of future is zesty, not heady. More biological, less theoretical. The vertical zodiac sings nature's most basic song of affirmation: "I will relate, grow and thrive."

No sooner did I arrange the zodiac to look like a plant reaching for the sun then did the true shape of the plant emerge: the torus field. The torus flows in a spiraling motion.

Though we will be exploring the toroscope in planetary pairs, I wish to make it known that there is an order from sign to sign. Taurus flows to Gemini, then to Virgo, then to Libra and so on.

As I continued to observe this new "map", more and more secrets of nature emerged. My reflection on what I found is the substance of this book. I hope you find these ideas as nourishing and renewing as I do.

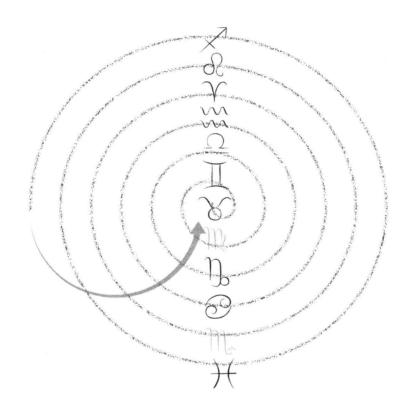

Spirited Nature

Taurus

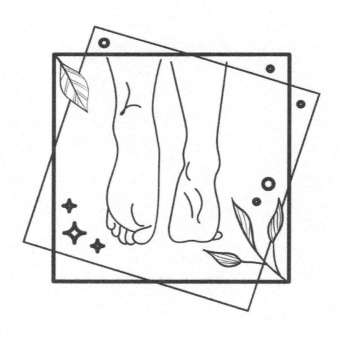

Chapter one

Natural science is the science of nature. But- What is nature?
Alfred North Whitehead

When my boy was learning to walk we spent many a summer afternoon at the park. I appreciated the softness of the grass cushioning fall after fall. I was happy to live in Vermont with such robust greenery. I got in the habit of kicking off my shoes. This is when I started to really wonder about the earth's powers.

The bliss of baby-rearing comes with its share of hassle, as any parent knows. It would never cease to amaze me that my feet on the soft sunny grass would inspire an instinct to skip and frolic. I'm in my forties in this grass and I can't help but frolic a bit. The baby gives me a carte blanche to galavant without raising eyebrows. Geo laughs and falls and springs up again. The delight snowballs bigger and brighter.

Some days I would wait to take off my shoes. I would observe "nope, i don't want to frolic" and then take my shoes off to instantly feel the opposite. I felt like a fly that was tired and lethargic until brought back into the natural air where it zipped off. There is magic in the earth. It can't be any other way. But could the magic also be in us, *shared with the earth*? My feet would seem to be sprung from the earth, as if I transformed into an earth elf! It was so notable that my favorite times were when I was feeling tense and then instantly released into my natural elven state.

I had heard much about grounding, and how walking without shoes was beneficial to one's health. I had heard this for years but it took a summer of feeling it for myself to be convinced. I thought about Tesla's insistence that the earth had plenty of free energy.[4]

Sitting on the earth continues to educate me. Its potency is so humbling. It is the most natural cue for me to bring my hands together, as if in prayer. For this seems to complete a circuit. The potency flows through me. Grounding me into feeling more free, more potent and more at peace. It is the perfect prayer. What potency or power could be more assuring to turn to when in need than this shared potency one has with nature?

Einstein said that if he believed in God then it was "Spinoza's God".[5] Baruch Spinoza was a 17th century philosopher who saw god to be one and the same as the singular "substance" of nature. A place beyond form. The only place of oneness.[6]

In the zodiac, the sign that represents nature is Taurus. Ruled by beautiful Venus, Taurus represents the bounty of the earth. It should come now as no surprise that it sits sturdily at the center of our torus (Taurus) field. Nature is robust. Nature is a torus field; the substance of all which includes god. It is a living, breathing organism of which we are all a part of. Therefore, nature is primary. Mind and thinking comes *after* nature.

Philosopher Owen Barfield sees consciousness evolving with a shift from the inside to the outside. Primitive man's thoughts were, as he called it an "original participation";[7] an immediate experience inside the world's unity. We used to be on the inside of nature, as the plants and animals are, but we are now outside of it. When we think, we think *about* something, and the very definition of about is "to be outside of".

Symbolically speaking, a bite from Eden's apple banished Adam and Eve from nature's full embrace. In an act of free-will, they separated from Taurus' field and embarked on a new kind of existence. The 'fall' was necessary to gain more freedom, for a fall anticipates a rise. Humans are free-thinkers with an adventurous road ahead.

Our reflective species is built to rise; to know nature with full consciousness, and thus become nature, *create nature*. It follows that we should create systems that will further sustain our mutual flourishing.

I am inclined to see the curved line atop of Taurus' symbol to be a smile. The smile flashes forth the upwardness of spirit. The upwardness of spirit is the tug of evolution, an urge to grow and become.

A smile is a "yes". I also am inclined to see "yes" to be a world, like the poet E.E. Cummings wrote. "yes is a world & in this world of yes live (skilfully curled) all worlds".[8] The world of yes is the health of nature. It is the true bounty from which we draw, the realest of banks.

The world of yes is bigger than yes and no. It is a celebration, like the light of fireflies. The world of yes buzzes with action and bustles with activity. There is no world of no. Only a world of yes and no. The world of yes and no serves the world of yes. A no that is virtuous is always in the name of a yes, or a value. Within the fortitude of a no lies the robust affirmation of a yes. One of the things that makes us human is our ability to say no for the sake of yes, in other words to take a stand for our beliefs and values.

A robust affirmation lies at nature's center. It knows "yes" in the most direct fashion because it connects to spirit, represented by Sagittarius. The arrow of evolution drives the smile into nature. The arrow knows the way, and it talks through the language of yes. The body continues to evolve in the name of yes, and knowing yes. The future of yes is to further create the beauty of yes.

This may sound far fetched. But I assure you, it is close by. Deep in your body you are rich. The bank is eternal. It never runs dry. Centering yourself is about tuning into the wash of your own activity, the hum of your own cricket meadow. Bruce Lee said that true stillness is stillness in movement.[2] There is nothing sterile about true stillness. True stillness is a conscious embrace of your own momentum. How is it flowing? Does it need redirection?

True stillness is an ownership of your own bustle. The bustle includes everything from how you talk to what you dream to what you love to what you fear. The activity of the cricket meadow doesn't come close to the activity of your own psyche. But can you hear the harmony? The peace? Can you shape it so it better invigorates you? Can you live in the world of yes while using the tools of yes and no? These are nature's questions.

Taurus holds within it the power of "aura", a force that radiates. A healthy aura affirms its own "livingness"; its own motion and peace. Venus, the smiling love goddess, is Taurus' archetype. This is a goddess who causes flowers to sprout from the ground that she walks on. The romantic element of Venus comes down to one powerful word: "relating". It is only through relating that life can grow and sustain itself.

Philosopher Josef Pieper wrote "a world is a field of relations". To have a world means "to be the center, the coordinator of a field of relations". The flowers have their worlds. They coordinate the water from the earth, drinking it in through their roots. They coordinate their sunlight, turning it into food. The animals have their worlds. They coordinate their own foraging of food and securing of shelter with all kinds of different environments.

The world of yes is pure instinct to the daisy and the bear. They navigate their fields beautifully and the result is the power of nature: the ongoing movement of many creatures in one world.

What about *your world*? In your world, time doesn't just turn, it also burns. Your world includes all of your memories and education, your hopes and dreams, your connections to others and to ideas. Your world is *your field*, your Taurus field.

Deep in the heart of your own nature, you coordinate this world. Your world should never be confused with your environment, for it is far fuller, wider and deeper. You are the coordinator. What power you have.

A flower draws water from the depths of the earth as you draw from your memory of what has come before. It turns to the light of the sun as you turn towards the light of meaning and hope. The mechanics of nature are consistent.

I began to think about the many other buzzwords of Taurus, and how they could further illuminate this "center of nature". There are words like business, wealth, health and ownership. Words like bounty, status-quo, beauty and taste. Indeed the whole world of aroma and flavor is represented by Taurus. It is a rich and textured sign.

What do you own? What is your business? What is your bounty, your taste and your beauty? How should you seek your profit?

Immediately we run into a problem. For there is another big and powerful word that is associated with Taurus: money. For a species that sometimes says "time is money", this is a force to be reckoned with. Although in reality, it isn't a force at all.

Philosopher Erich Fromm has written at length about the downfalls of an overly consumerist society. In his book *To Have Or To Be* he says that there are two basic existential modes of living, the "having mode" and the "being mode". The having mode is about possessing and consuming whereas the being mode is about "an authentic relating to the world". He sees a downward spiraling of a society that focuses too much on the "having mode" and not enough on the "being mode".[10]

Fromm asserts that humans are not only social and rational creatures but "producing" ones as well and that "living productively" is the only true path to happiness.[11]

This rings a bell for me. I see in my mind an apple tree, a bountiful tree displaying the beauty of its producing nature. If I reflect on when I am happiest, it's easy to see that I am happiest when I am in a"fruitful" state of mind. I feel at my best when I'm in a productive mode of being, or more accurately, a productive flow of 'becoming'.

Productive might mean staying up all night to get ahead with one's work, or making the best Halloween costume for your child, but it also means something more simple. A fruitful state of mind carries with it a healthy attitude of "readiness". As you engage with others, or things, or places there is *a readiness for something new to emerge.* This is a kinship with your own alchemy. It is an enjoyment of your capacity to relate authentically to others, situations, ideas and things. It isn't a blind sense of optimism, it is *rooted* in reality: the reality of your own productive and creative powers.

For if reality is to be the full reality it must include spiritedness, and ultimately it is spiritedness that sustains life and keeps it growing. There would be no 'reality' if it weren't for spiritedness. We would have died out a long time ago if the powers of growth ceased their processes. Yet many self-proclaimed 'realists' are ready to dismiss the primacy of spirit in the name of what can be proven, that is to say in favor of certainty.

Yet as Erich Fromm says "the quest for certainty blocks the search for meaning. Uncertainty is the very condition to impel man to unfold his powers. If he faces the truth without panic he will recognize that *there is no meaning to life except the meaning man gives his life by the unfolding of his powers, by living productively*"[12] (his italics)

For Fromm, the only certainty that existed was the "certainty that grows from productive activity." The ownership of this certainty is very real. No one can take this away. It is yours and it is unique because you are unique.

Our consumerist society has also shifted to an "under ownership" society, with "services" replacing "things." Your unique and productive nature can never be replaced. You can put full trust in it. You can have what Fromm called "rational faith." He says that faith is "the conviction of the not yet proven, the knowledge of the real possibility, the awareness of pregnancy."

Ahh pregnancy. I loved being pregnant. I loved the secret of his hiccups while I sat at the front desk of a doctor's office checking in patients. I loved the embrace, the movement from within and the dreams that they inspired.

When he joined us in the 'real world' I continued to enjoy a sense of pregnancy. This pregnancy however was psychological, even spiritual. It was the pregnancy of a moment. My senses were wide open to his perfection. How he moved his mouth, his eyes. How he used his hands and feet. His wonderful little voice. His force field. Each moment was pregnant and fertile with possibility. The air of discovery blended with the magic of the Christmas Season. I remember stepping silently down the hospital halls with socks too big. Baskets of chocolates and Christmas lights were on display here and there. And then there was the treasure: him, my little boy. The happiness was so wholesome, so complete, and so effervescent. I understand this to be an absolute conscious embrace of nature.

Sagittarius is the sign of faith. It dives into nature (Taurus) and begins a lifelong churning process. Fire lights up the earth, as seen in a flower's vibrant color, an animal's swiftness, or a person's smile. Why do we dance, laugh and 'shake it off?' It is because we are spirited by design. Rigidity is a fast path away from evolution. Mechanization is for the insects. Though we create and use many machines, we were never intended to become machine-like.

Faith and spiritedness are both Sagittarian terms, ruled by buoyant Jupiter. If you flip Jupiter's glyph upside down it becomes the glyph of Saturn, or rationality. Rationality and faith are mirror images of each other in a healthy torus-field, as is law and freedom, integrity and bliss, effort and hope. There is strength in marrying your contractive and sobering forces with your expansive forces of hope and enthusiasm. These are but some of the preliminary teachings of the toroscope. To go further we must open our eyes, into the world of perception. We must awaken to the laws of the mind.

Perceiving

Gemini and Virgo

Chapter two

The intuitive mind is a sacred gift and the rational mind is a faithful servant.
We have created a society that honors the servant and has forgotten the gift.
Albert Einstein

The mind has two signs, Gemini and Virgo, outer air and inner earth.

Gemini's side perceives the many many things, thoughts and stimuli of the world around us. Its archetype is the twins because everything we encounter, perceive or think about becomes a brief and fleeting twinship. For there is no divorcing the observer from the observed.

Virgo's archetype is the Virgin who tends to the fields. Her work is so ingrained (no pun intended) that she herself is part of the field, that is the field of experience. Her earthiness, her flesh and biochemistry respond to these fleeting twinships. She sends surges of biofeedback that affirm or negate the many many partnerships at play.

Encircling the fertility of nature is mind. Mind perceives outward and inward stimulus. Mythology describes Mercury to be a trickster god who travels swiftly between worlds. He is a trickster for he can't reveal the full reality of the world. To do so would decentralize the self, and bombard the senses with too much information. Mercury does better to speak in riddles with a tongue in cheek. The fibonacci that our eyes perceive in a sunflower is like the smile on a Sphynx. The beauty draws us in and a sense of mystery pervades the air. The subtext of someone's words is better heard with the help of a compassionate heart. Our perceptions are messages delivered deep into our spirited nature.

Ideas, and images enter into our organisms and change us. We are in a constant state of reflection and creation. The quicksilvered god never stops offering up information. The information germinates our fertile ground continuously.

Neuroscientist Antonio Damasio not only defines consciousness to be "a mind with a self in it" he also says that our idea of self is continuously arising from what the mind grapples with. The organism encounters an "object".[13] It could be a thought, a thing, a person, a sound, a feeling or any other stimulus. In engaging with this object, the object changes the organism and an idea of self is created. Because the mental imagery never runs out, the idea of self is continuous. This is Gemini's twinship; its 'stream of consciousness'.

We are two. We are the organism and the object. Our ideas of self are continuously generated from the interplay of 'other' and 'ourselves'.

I have always been intrigued by talk about the left and right brain. The left brain is said to be logical, "i-dotting" and best able to cope with the demands of a day. The right brain is said to be more of an artist that synthesizes a big picture. The right brain emerges in times of relaxation.

Maybe it is all the Virgo that I have in my own birth chart, but I crave a steady dose of relaxed contemplation. One of my favorite pastimes is reading a book next to some sunlit water with a cup of coffee. The waves of wellbeing wash over me as I encounter new morsels of interest to digest. The discovery in the air makes peace in my body. Sunlight dances upon the page and the water. Who knows what kinds of dreams awaken.

I crave this feeling, and I try to make room for it. Writing is an excellent strategy. But sometimes my writing time is more 'forced' than 'delighted in'. I read back what I wrote and it sounds mechanical. I go through a stretch of not looking forward to writing. I can't imagine not looking forward to reading my book by sunny water, why does this happen with writing?

Colin Wilson became an overnight success with his first book, *The Outsider* in 1952. His work develops an existentialism rooted in optimism, unlike the pessimistic slant of most existential writings (take Sartre's "man is a useless passion" or "hell is other people"). Among the mechanics of consciousness that he explores is the relationship between the left and right brain.

The problem, as Wilson sees it, is that these two sides are too often in conflict where there should be close cooperation. He says that we are "stranded in the left brain." The logical side of us that must deal with external events everyday is our sense of "I".[14] We lose complete touch with the restorative powers of the "artist who lives in the shadows"[15] which is the right brain. What a pity! This is exactly what I feel when I'm out of sync with my writing.

He talks about the reaction a caveman might have to seeing all the luxury of modern life. The caveman would likely think that at last humankind can relax and enjoy the fruits of existence. But we aren't! We continue to fetter ourselves and get bored. On a whole we are not stopping to smell the roses or taking a moment to sit by the dock of the bay. We are a stressed out species. For Wilson, this problem can only be solved by considering the *right relationship between the left and right brain.*

In the toroscope, the left brain is Gemini, a process of twinship with every 'other' we encounter (a person, thing, thought). Gemini is the one in control. It summons the powers of the right brain. Virgo is the right brain, the artist at work who constantly tends to the field of which she is a part. We have to call the artist into play with a mental effort. Otherwise we can be stranded forever in the left brain, completely unaware of the *potential of our whole mind.* Gemini's twinships can be empty if they do not summon the animating and vital energies of Virgo's field.

To put this idea into better focus, here is an example that Wilson gives about the two sides of the brain at work with his own writing habits. He explains that the first few pages he writes are laborious and difficult because he is only writing with his left brain. He is 'sawing a double handled saw by himself'. But after a bit of effort he feels 'someone has taken up the other end'.[16] His right brain has joined in, and the rest of the writing flows smoothly and naturally.

I have noticed the same phenomenon myself. The best part is that I can come to depend on the emergence of my right brain.

The mutual reinforcement of each side of the brain working together is charming. It reminds me of these chipmunks in a cartoon who are constantly polite to each other. The left brain puts forth a sentence and the right brain delights to add something extra. The left brain says thank you and the right brain says your welcome.

I have a twin sister. We have said that these polite chipmunks remind us of ourselves. Perhaps my craving for the "whole mind" comes from a deep well of ancestral dreams. And then voila, there we are: two polite chipmunks in a womb together, waiting to be born and talk to each other.

The mind is only whole when Gemini and Virgo cooperate. Your Geminian interests and mental efforts summon the earthy artist from the shadows. A natural sense of Virgoan leisure sneaks in. It is lovely to begin to trust in this process. Your poor left brain is assisted at last by the enormous and *animating powers of synthesis*. It does wonders for writing but it also does wonders for everyday living. It evokes the true spirit of leisure, which, according to philosopher Josef Pieper, is essential to preserving the dignity of human beings.

In his book, *Leisure as the Basis of Culture*, Pieper writes that the ancient Greek word for leisure was "skole" which produced the Latin word "scola" which produced the English word "school".[17] This was also their word for learning institutions. Schools were settings of leisure and places of celebrative contemplation. There were no competitive deadlines, no hurried eating.

Leisure leads to great discoveries, from Galileo watching a pendulum swing in a cathedral to Archimedes jumping out of his bathtub yelling "Eureka!". If we discount its importance in our lives we run the risk of thwarting our own evolution, on a grand scale and a personal one.

Pieper warns about the dangers of the workaday world, and how it can attempt to sabotage the 'real world'; a world that includes spirit. He writes, "The really human thing is to see the stars above the roof, to preserve our apprehension of the universality of things in the midst of the habits of our daily life, and to see "the world" above and beyond our immediate environment." [18]

Gemini represents a uniquely human phenomenon: the birth of reflective thought. As Pierre Teilhard de Chardin said, "man came silently into this world". With its symbol of the twins, Gemini represents the split from nature's unity to pave the path of human evolution. We have become free, but why? What is it that we are *free for?*

The ease of Virgoan leisure could be likened to being a bit drunk. Colin Wilson says "A cow is so contented in a field because it's drunk!"[19] Like all animals, the cow is inside of nature's unity, flowing like the rivers and the breezes.

When Virgo comes in to complete Gemini's divided mind, our natures awaken. The magic in the air comes forth and fresh energy stirs. Would it be right to assume that evolution leads to a big glass of wine? Enough wine might make the stars brighter but as any responsible driver knows, it inhibits your sense of control and focus. An athlete would never show up to a match half drunk because it would ruin his game. But the athlete, in his flow state will still be engaging with his full mind. He will walk back into the garden of Eden, so to speak, fully awake. With every focused move he will encounter the immediate feedback of his efforts. This according to author Mihaly Csikszentmihalyi is a crucial component of the 'flow state'. He writes, "Most enjoyable activities are not natural; they demand an effort that initially one is reluctant to make. But once the interaction starts to provide feedback to the person's skills, it usually begins to be intrinsically rewarding."[20]

The left brain summons the brightness of the stars by awakening the energies of the right brain. Gemini's real role is to be curious and attentive enough to bring in the animism of the full mind. Virgo has been labeled many things but it is seldom labeled a drunk. The leisure of Virgo is induced by an awake and interested mind.

Contemplative moods should be encouraged for the well-being of the whole person. The mind, left to its own devices (especially modern ones) will go about in a dizzying addiction to 'splitting things' and multitasking. Left out of Gemini's fun, Virgo might fall asleep. That's when Gemini stops having fun, often unbeknownst to the owner of the mind. Obsessive email-checking is normalized by society. The artist retreats back to the shadows.

Pythagoras envisioned the universe to be composed entirely of right angles. Rightness is embedded in the body. This is why saying 'yes' when you want to dance with someone fills you with wonderful flutters and why abrupt rudeness can turn your stomach. Virgo reverberates the 'right angles' of the cosmos from within the body. She is like an unstruck bell. Gemini is the idea, the thought or the 'thing' that strikes the bell. The resonance that comes forth brings the grand synthesis of the full mind, or the cosmos within.

There is logic to an optimistic mindset. When one is in an optimistic state of mind, the two sides of the brain are more likely to help eachother out. Gemini, the left brain is receptive to the artistic suggestions of Virgo, the right brain. Virgo, the right brain, rushes in to celebrate and enhance the interesting things that Gemini finds. But it is always Gemini who is in control. The interest of Gemini summons the energy of Virgo.

It is important to remember that we identify with Gemini. When we say "I" we are identifying with the left brain, the logical linguistic side of us that copes with external events.

But there is another "I" to recognize. We must practice reminding ourselves of the constant presence of our right brain, though it may fall asleep when bored. What is important is knowing that Virgo is there, ready to send surges of positive biofeedback in response to our focus and interest in things. It is not so much a matter of always striving for right brain awareness as it is keeping close the knowledge that she is always there. We can put trust in her. We can put trust in that artist that lives in the shadows. We can see the logic of an optimistic mindset, as well as the logic in searching for things that we find interesting and worth caring about.

When Descartes revolutionized philosophy with the words "I think therefore I am" he also paved for it a dead end road. The left brain became all there is. The mysteries of synthesis provided by the right brain became mere 'subjectivity', not to be heeded as anything *real*. The nature within us became discounted, not worthy of exploring. All that could be known for sure was that which 'facts' could prove. But the first fact was full of error. *Mind is not the beginning.* It follows a spirited nature. It doesn't create the self, it serves the self. It exists to further illuminate nature and create more nature and more light. The mind's capacity for discovery goes far beyond the 'facts'.

The mind is a key with potential to unlock the stirrings of nature. All of our senses connect us to the movement, the buzz, the production. Yet, as the Earth Spirit warns Faust, "your senses sleep." It becomes all too easy to pass on this symphony, and take no heed to its teachings. And then the boredom sets in, along with anxiety. This is for good reason. The mind does best when used purposefully, that is to say when the two sides cooperate.

The bounty of a full mind is extremely accessible. All that is needed is a readiness to be interested in the things around you. What truly interests you? If you can find some good answers to this question you can look forward to a most enjoyable thing.

You can anticipate the arrival of your latent mental energies. Who knows how long they have been asleep! Months? Years? Decades? If you have gone on long enough without considering what it is that most interests you then odds are that your senses sleep!

Your metabolism sleeps. For these latent mental energies are born from the earth, from your body and its team of interrelated life. Microbes outnumber human cells ten to one. Virgo's energy comes from nature, *is nature.* Heightened interest and care animates your field and makes your meadow of crickets sing. To 'burn time' is to come alive in your relations, and wake up to the powers that lie dormant within.

What comes next in this process of time metabolism? After the mind with a self in it? After consciousness?

Engaging

Libra and Capricorn

Chapter three

The only person you are destined to become is the person you decide to be.
Ralph Waldo Emerson

Libra and Saturn introduce the seasons of Fall and Winter. The leaves on the trees turn red, orange and yellow. They no longer recede into the distance as green scenery. They advance into focus. We are inspired to pick up a fallen leaf and look closer at it. Winter is cold. We draw our energies in, stay inside, cook hot food and hunker down. Winter is a time of collecting our vital energies inward. The zodiac wheel turns and educates us. In knowing the seasons we know ourselves.

What happens when we draw our energies in? What kinds of things come forward and prompt us to bring them closer yet? What happens when we focus our energies into something other, something worthy of our focus?

The fall leaves are brilliant in color. The winter is sobering with its chill. Beauty beckons us forth to get serious and sober about things. Something that is 'worth our time' can lead to a lifelong commitment. That which fascinates can *draw us in*. Our energies contract and enter into that which fascinates. We become a part of it.

Nature is capable of displaying great works of beauty. The complex design of a butterfly wing is also simple with divine laws of proportion. It is not a 'loud shirt' with random color schemes. It is ordered; ordered by something wonderful that underlies all creation. The beauty of the butterfly wing is like the beauty of our own bodies with our seashell-like ears and our galaxy-like eyes. Throughout history, artists have been quick to recognize a sacred pattern to nature's beautiful expression. It is known as the golden ratio; nature's divine signature of proportion.

Artists like Leonardo Da Vinci and Michelangelo would work the precision of nature's mathematics into their masterpieces. The divine beauty that emerged was rooted in natural law. Heaven, as they could prove, is here on earth, by grace of these sacred proportions and relations. In knowing the formula of nature, with all of its divinity, one has the capacity to create natural divinity, or real beauty.

The golden ratio, otherwise known as phi or the fibonacci sequence, shows the pattern of nature as it grows. One plus one brings us to two. Two plus one to three. Three plus two to five and so on. The relation between each step is one of accumulation. The next step marries itself to what has come before. The growth pattern is a spiral. Nothing is wasted. All is incorporated into the design.

For a rose, there is no doubt about how to continue growing and expanding. There is no confusion of a sense of self. The result is nothing short of a visible and tangible divinity.

Human beings are sometimes blessed with plenty of physical beauty. For some of us, the ratios are Boticelli-like, and we can thank the lottery of our genetics. But a pretty face will soon disappoint if an attitude non-supportive to growth reveals itself, such as cynicism and shallowness. For this is a lack of spiritedness which is unnatural and therefore not beautiful.

Before birth, we are perfect little seashell swirls in our mother's womb. From birth on, our bodies continue to grow in the divine spirit of nature. And then they stop growing. What does this mean in terms of this divine process? Do our own 'masterpieces' stop 'becoming'?

Michelangelo studied the laws of growing in order to produce beauty. If we want to produce beauty in our lives we too must learn these laws of growing. This is the essence of Libra and Capricorn. This spiral deals with learning nature's laws, so that you can produce more nature, more beauty and more bounty.

We are just like the rose that grows by 'marrying itself to what has come before.' The rose delights in the full affirmation of the sun. What is free is necessary and what is necessary is free. Within its unity with nature there is no agency, no ability to control its future. For the rose, 'future' is only biological growing. The future of the rose is the same thing as its growingness, or its health.

We grow, but we are also free agents. Our worlds are wider and deeper. They include our rich inner lives and visions to plan our futures. We can envision ourselves in an imagined future and we can reflect on ourselves in a remembered past. This is how we are infinitely *more related to our own growing* than the rose. We share the same laws with the rose, but unlike the rose we can come to know these laws and embrace them creatively. We can apply the laws of growth to vision, reflection, and planning. We can encourage a healthy fibonacci pattern by being honest enough with *what came before* so we can consciously *marry some freedom into something new.*

Let's say that you are stuck in a rut at a dead end job. Each day is a glom and a struggle. You are beginning to lose your sense of self and your ability to enjoy your life. It is only in being completely honest with yourself about where you are that you can steer your toroidal ship. You can't get to Disneyland if you don't first understand yourself to be in Kansas.

The misery of the job must be confronted with a focused sobriety. You must figure out the real reasons why you are miserable. Are the people unpleasant? Are you working too many hours? Did you ever like the job? Did something change? The one thing that you know is that right now you are miserable. The question becomes: what do you want to marry this misery with? More misery? A realistic strategy to make things better? A change of course? A change of attitude?

I had a job that I didn't like for a few months right when I became pregnant. I was put "on the phones" at a doctors' office along with a big staff in a windowless room. My head was chained to the headset, my eyes glued to the computer screen. My fingers were tense from typing at warp speed. The worst of it was the people on the other end of the phone were often so rude. They didn't have to look me in the eye. I was just the voice that answered when they'd been waiting "forever!" I ended the day often in tears. I worried constantly about my sadness affecting the world of my baby, who was a secret to me at work for I was not yet showing. Everyday I would take my lunch break in the park down the road reading existential books by Neitzche and Rollo May, desperate to find *a better way.*

And then one day it came to me in a flash. I understood what the root of my misery was: a lack of light and nature. I understood that I needed some daylight and human connection to be happy at work. These are things I had before in other job positions. I never knew they were so central to my own well-being.

I confronted my boss saying that I just couldn't do it anymore. To my surprise she said "no problem, we will put you at the front desk!" The next day I was sitting in the sunshine greeting people and looking them in the eye. My baby bump began to show and I bought cute maternity dresses to be presentable in my new and visible place. I loved these days. I felt so much more alive. And it all came from a realistic assessment of my misery *married to a new plan.*

In the zodiac, Libra is beauty and Saturn is effort. Many great works of art reveal a hidden story of enormous effort. The deep peace and relaxation that art can induce is a wonderful complement to the effort one made to create it. A whole small town can enjoy the most delicious strawberries from the efforts of one farmer. The efforts that you deem worthy of your taking can create lots of beauty, not just for your own life but for many others too.

The order that is created in nature and by nature comes from a most spirited place. As we learned in the beginning, Taurus' field is spirited. The sign Taurus in the middle is our sense of self. Our selves, our natures are ruled by Venus, the beautiful one who *relates*. Taurus connects and draws from the spiritedness of Sagittarius, with all of its giddy hope and freedom.

Sagittarius is ruled by Jupiter, the flipped glyph of Saturn. The giddiness and bliss of Sagittarius is but the mirror-image of Saturn's serious endeavors. Effort is the flipside of hope, spiritedness and belief. Efforts spark the spirit and spirit inspires effort. Beauty grows as you grow. The bounty is true to who you are. Striving and hoping go hand in hand.

Just like love and life, nature is best understood as a verb. Nature *is* productivity. To be natural is to embrace a fruitful mindset and help grow what is good and beautiful.

The springy goodness that my feet detected from the earth that summer is but the fibonacci in waiting. It is the spirit of growth (Jupiter) whereas the butterfly wing reveals its external expression (Saturn). The spirit is invisible and potent. It is to be felt individually though it is also shared with all of nature. It is nature. It is the spirit of growing that connects everyone to everyone else. A spirited message within the seashell and the pinecone will sneak into our subconscious if we spend enough time in nature. They will remind us of this grand design; a design that unites all living creatures through the spirit of growing and becoming.

Who knows the peace that the tamarin mother monkey feels after she has successfully out-jumped a cheetah from the trees with her twins on her back. Her spirit is fierce and ablaze with purpose. Her bounty is as tangible and actual as the rising sun. For the animal, life is a necessary adventure.

Saturn's efforts for a bounty worth striving for is a ticket to adventure. Think about your own life. Where have you put forth a lot of effort? What bounty does it show? Is it beautiful like a sunflower? Is it still invisibly stirring beneath the earth? What efforts do you see your loved ones around you engaged in? What bounties? Can you draw inspiration from them?

Your recognition of beauty affirms your deepest sense of self which is a spirited and creative nature. Beauty stirs your most natural instinct to relate wholeheartedly. It is only by such wholehearted relating that you can come to know your productive powers. The bliss of spirit expands while the commitment to creating contracts.

Creativity is not just about painting pictures and making music, though these are wonderful examples. It is more about striving for perfection. Abraham Maslow said "A first-rate soup is more creative than a second-rate painting." He personally noticed the amazing creativity of his stepmother who could make the house look and smell wonderful with very little money. For example, he remembers her assembling twigs in a jar for added elegance to the dining table.

Beauty is always within reach, to inspire, guide or remind you of your true identity. There is a reality found in nature that speaks through beauty and design to the reality of the spirit.

So far the toroscope has revealed an inner certainty of productive potential with Taurus and Sagittarius. Gemini and Virgo have introduced the mechanics of mind with the left summoning the animating powers of the right. And then there is beauty. Beauty surrounds and awaits. As for time-metabolism, the question becomes; will you connect with the beauty? Will you engage with something and strive to create? Might you even commit to something and put forth your focus and efforts?

Connecting with beauty inspires a gathering of the potency within us. We focus ourselves into the beauty. A natural commitment ensues to creating beauty, bounty or goodness. Saturn's integrity is a wonderful feeling. It brings about a kind of sturdiness that speaks to the real essence of living. As Emerson said "Life is not intellectual or critical, but sturdy".[21]

I have felt the bliss of Saturn find me on the worst of days. There is no comparison to this feeling. It confirms that you have collected yourself and turned to the light of hope and action instead of away from it. It confirms your right to be rational and creative just as you were designed.

Venus and Saturn anchor us to reality through the virtue of well-being. Rational decisions foster well-being, be it our own or the well-being of others. There is no divorcing well-being from rationality. Rationality refers to what is in someone's best interest.

As conscious and rational creatures we are a species that must cooperate in order to thrive. As the poet Gwendolyn Brooks said "We are each other's harvest; we are each other's business; we are each other's magnitude and bond".[22] Your own well-being is bound up with the well-being of others.

The Mercuries speak to the importance of a heightened interest. Our curiosity unlocks the latent powers of our natures. Our full body mind awakens in the light of something worth considering or investigating. But this could go on forever in a way not conducive to our flourishing if it weren't for rationality. An interest in scuba diving could put one in danger if a rational mind didn't grapple with basic safety measures that are needed.

I see nature's beauty as similar to the spirit of Mary Poppins. She brings about magic, fun and surprise yet she also teaches proper conduct. A spoonful of sugar is blended with an upright attitude. A seriousness heightens the engagement of the game.

If it weren't for the horizons of Libra and the fortitude of Capricorn, life would be nothing but a series of mind games. Gemini would find interests and Virgo would animate the body, but it wouldn't *lead anywhere.* Not only would there be no great civilizations or works of literature, there would be no laws, no marriages, no schools, no upbringings of children.

Gemini is the first date, the first flash of the smile. But Libra's horizon of 'what could come of this' is what makes one 'walk the Capricornian line'.

Let's say that you have Venus placed in Aries and Saturn in Virgo. You will likely find beauty in Aries-like things;

adventure, independence, maybe competitive sports. This affinity summons an upright attitude that needs a code of conduct. Saturn in Virgo answers with Virgo-like strategy; routines, healthy eating, long stretches of contemplation. Who knows the nuance of how this might blend in a person. They could be serious competitive athletes, or maybe they make adventure a routine, or maybe their independence is fostered by long stretches of contemplation. The permutations are endless because we are talking about an individual person with subtleties of character that go on and on. But, as an individual, considering these combinations in a strategic way is most certainly in their best interest! Who knew astrology could be so rational.

In our efforts to engage we create ourselves anew. For Venus is the heart of us and also the horizon before us. Beauty awaits our discovery.

Productivity guru David Allen talks about the importance of "appropriate engagement". He says "your mind is for having ideas, not holding them".[23] When the mind tries to hold on to many ideas at once we find ourselves only half engaged with the task at hand. And sometimes the task at hand might really need appropriate engagement, like when a child is asking for guidance.

'Appropriate' is a Saturn word, and 'engagement' is a Venus word. Indeed these two ideas are the ultimate marriage yet its message is so easy to lose sight of. Just as the artists followed the formality of the golden ratio to create staggering works of beauty, one must *follow some formality in their relations if they care to see them grow.* In the commitment to engaging appropriately to what you deem worthy or beautiful, you also grow your own nature along with the bounty.

To be engaged is sacred. It doesn't bode well with distractions. We find ourselves now in a highly distracted digital world. Saturn is also a comfortability with solitude; a kind of stillness to be called upon in order to see things as they *really are.*

In his book, Man For Himself, Erich Fromm points out that to be objective when relating to something does not mean to be devoid of emotion. It simply means 'respecting' that which you relate to as its own entity, and not adding anything to it. For 'respect' comes from the root 'respicere' which means 'to look at'. It's the "ability to see a person as he is, to be aware of his individuality and uniqueness."[24]

Scientific observation shares much with the formalities of a square dance. The respect for things as they are is what supports real and objective observation, and therefore *real relating*. Real relationships are not built on illusion, they are built on respect.

The problem many people find themselves in today is a lack of solitude and privacy. The digital world has made us more connected on a grand scale but it has also made our minds noisier. This digital noise can leak into our everyday sacred relations. It dings and beckons us away from a natural instinct *to go deeper with something*; a thought, an activity, a beholding of beauty. Just before we can focus ourselves appropriately and feel our integrity take a nice solid shape, our phones jerk us back into the shallows of a fragmented and far less real reality. The digital world is a wonderful tool, a wide world of interesting avenues of thinking and connecting, but it is up to us to install within it some rules of engagement.

It is up to you and you alone to keep your engagements appropriate. This mandate comes from your nature's best interest. Arguing it is like arguing about a healthy diet. If there are things that are worth your time and relating, then do it right.

There is a certain crystalline world to treasure. A three dimensional molecular and texturized world full of aroma and color. The engagement of a farmer in the field, or a person reading something highly interesting is a fuller engagement than scrolling an endless social feed.

There is a romance to reality, but not if we forget to respect what we encounter, and engage with it appropriately. These beautiful engagements are what inspires us to contract in a most healthy way, and discover something realer than real: our own light from within.

Navigating

Aquarius and Cancer

Chapter four

Man does not yet exist. Colin Wilson

This book was nearly finished when the Full Moon came. It was a perfect late summer night and the Moon was full in Pisces. Harry, my partner, and I snuck down the driveway to get a better peak at its beauty. Unobscured by trees and mingling with fog appeared a most perfect glowing Moon. We made a fire on our back deck. The crackling of the fire further syncopated the wash of crickets in the meadow below. The light of the fire grew with the light of the moon. Harry is an especially electric Cancer, so he always adds even more buzz to a buzzing scene. At a Mets game he once gave an electric shock to a man as he reached out to accept a bag of pretzels. It was loud, and the man yelled "Yeeeow!".

In all of this buzzing, peaceful bustle I realized that I would rewrite the book. For the peaceful bustle is as close a metaphor as I can find to nature. By the light of the moon I was changed and impelled to also *make a change.*

This is the power of this next spiral; Aquarius and Cancer. These two signs deal with the undefinable and ever-present; the 'now' that is forever escaping our grasp. We have come to the threshold of existence itself.

Existence is an elusive concept to say the least. It is defined as a state of living but this is misleading because the 'state' is continuously and constantly changing. It is much better defined as *a way of living*. It could even be called a path. Existence is very zen.

A popular zen question asks: if a tree falls in a forest but no one is around, would it make a sound? The toroscope reveals an opinion: yes it would.

Existence, like everything else in the toroscope, is two-fold. There is both outer existence and inner existence. Both of these are in continuous flux. Uranus or Aquarius represents the flux of outer existence; the 'times that are a changin'. Cancer or the Moon represents inner existence; the rising and falling tides of our private feelings and chemistries.

Outer existence is the sound the tree *does* make when it falls in the forest with no one around. Inner existence comes from the person (had they been in the forest) that hears the sound, or even the person that wonders if a sound would be heard.

A full moon can stir things up and make existence more surely *felt*. The pleasant changes in my chemistry inspired changes in my thoughts. The changes in the scenery with the growing light and crackling chirping sounds stirred me in the same way that I could hear and see the stirrings of nature. For a nice and delicious stretch, outer existence and inner existence became completely harmonious. I felt embraced and guided. I felt a restful education, a most satisfying awakening. It seemed I was connected to my scenery in a lively and near electric way. There was a sharing of the moon's glow and the crickets activity. It was a bewitching experience.

I became certain of an idea: *deep peace is the height of activity; the thing that underlies all of nature's serenity is action.* The certainty led to a change of course, a kind of rerouting. I had to rewrite the book from this new 'center' of knowing.

It all of a sudden seemed obvious to me that it was fire, which could also be said to be agency, creativity, action or meaning, that is the basis for everything. But such a knowing is a deeply subjective and private discovery even though it unites you with the all of the all. Deep peace is dynamic with the awareness of both a definite separation as well as a complete union with nature, *as nature.* The paradox is welcomed, as well as an invitation to create.

Leo Tolstoy famously said "life is when tiny changes occur."

Tiny changes lead to big changes in history. The zeitgeist was something totally different in your grandparents' day. If humans were to be wiped out yet our information and libraries were still accessible, the zeitgeist could be restarted like an automobile in winter. It exists whether or not we do. Aquarius' wavy lines show the movement in the air from which we attempt to center ourselves. Cancer's whirlpool sign is Aquarius 'water that it bears'; drawing from the peripheries of the known world deep into a private center. Just as a whirlpool organizes the currents of water, or a tornado organizes the currents of air, our subjective centers organize the currents of experience.

Though they seem so far apart, the changes that occur in our deepest centers on any given day connect to the changes that shape our history. Some of our finest works of literature, scientific discovery and art come from individuals who grappled with how they became changed. Einstein was changed by his fascination with a compass his father gave him when he was only five years old.[25] Louis Armstrong's album "West End Blues" changed the chemistry of a twelve year old Billie Holiday between her duties of scrubbing halls in some neighborhood apartments.[26]

For some of us, a change can strike like lightning, polarizing us to a 'true north'. For most of us, it is the tiny changes that slowly build a magnetic force to orient towards. The changes that occur within are what motivates us to make changes. Affectivity is what inspires action. The shape shifting of the moon alludes to the capacity for us to shape shift our inner lives, and find our own *way*.

If Cancer's whirlpool is a private center that draws from the wavy movement of the 'changin times', how does this compare to Taurus, the robust center of nature?

Cancer's whirlpool draws the periphery of *the world as we know it* into a private center. Deep within the inner life, spiritedness is recognized. A glimmer flickers. Will it build into something bigger?

Taurus' center draws from the *full world*; a world that includes the reality of the spirit, the bigness of the spirit. For Taurus, spirit is assumed, not rebirthed. It isn't Taurus' job to recognize the spirit, it is Taurus' job to *store* the spirit, embody the spirit, and delight in such goodness. And there is always more spirit to be recognized, more light to be stored. What happens when you draw from a 'world of spiritedness'? What does a world of spiritedness even look like? "Holiday consciousness" is a term Colin Wilson employs to denote a special kind of awareness. It is "the feeling children experience when setting out on holiday. Expectation of interesting experiences arouses a flood of energy, 'the secret life', which makes it self evident that life is marvelously complex and fascinating."[27]

The world of spiritedness is a world in which one *recognizes magic* . The build of enthusiasm creates more magic. Once again this is most natural to children, but that is not to say that adults can't center themselves 'naturally' in the 'world of spirit'. Grown ups who have found a sense of purpose might see the world of spirit in the relationships they care about or in the perfection of the watermelons that they grow. Spirit is confirmed by the connection they have with their own progress, their own growing and the growing that they inspire.

For the child on a holiday, centering himself in the spirited world creates a feeling of magic that further creates the magic he encounters. Magic may seem a bit far away for adults. Does the grown up want to be centered on magic? Let's find a word that suits the grown up better yet doesn't stray from the truth of what is going on. The grown up who centers herself in a world of spirit *welcomes well-being.*

The natural, Taurean centering is a centering of well-being. For what is really happening for the child on a holiday but an overflow of well-being, a building up of happiness?

Now what about the other way; the moonlit path of private centering in an ever changing zeitgeist?

Well let me take you back to my night on the deck under the Full Pisces Moon. There is no doubt that this was a spirited world that found me that night. There is no doubt that what I experienced was a profound sense of well-being. The centering was most natural, but also most *private.*

The Full Moon spoke to the Moon in me, a place of continuous change. I registered this well-being, the dynamic and peaceful changes inside. And then *my well-being went more private with discovery.* It made me ask myself "what do I want to do with this feeling?" In the deepest privacy of a question, an innerworld of spirit and adventure glow into sight, like an ember in the fire. In the privacy of a feeling I decided to change route. As far as the book was concerned, I found a *new center of gravity* from which to navigate.

In his book *Varieties of Religious Experience,* William James wrote that the religious man is not necessarily the man who has had the most religious experience but rather the man who makes religious experience *his center of gravity.* This center allows one to "sink into an attitude more stable."[28] This is a matter of *orientation.*

Because we are free inside, we can tune into and even *choose our centers of gravity.* Someone can choose the piano to be their center of gravity, along with other things like family and kindness. This is religious in nature but the 'church' is private, belonging only to the individual.

Well-being is the center of nature in a world of spirit. Nature is productive and so are we. Our private centering allows us to reflect on scenarios, past, present, and future to enhance our productive powers and *create a center that suits us best.* Some may call it ego, others may call it a north star, but the idea is the same; we can have a say in *what pulls us and how we want to navigate.*

We are living in the age of Aquarius, the water bearer. Also associated with technology, Aquarius shows the inventive side of human nature, the side that truly paves the way for the future. The search engine appears at our fingertips but it is also ingrained in our nature. An archetype associated with Aquarius is Prometheus, whose name means 'foresight'. We are searchers in the most natural sense. Choosing a center of gravity has to do with having foresight, that is to say searching and getting an idea about how to navigate one's life. As Sartre famously said, "everything has been figured out except how to live."

Arthur M. Young says that the inventor is someone who has learned the law, and then used the law to work for them. This understanding not only accompanied him throughout his ten year endeavor of creating the first commercial helicopter in 1945, it inspired much of his thinking as a cosmologist. Something particularly interesting that he noticed in creating the helicopter was how evolution works. He found that "without purpose, without a goal-directed activity, the helicopter could not possibly have evolved." He likened the assembly line to the building blocks of DNA.

"Evolution, it is supposed, is due to accidental mutations in the DNA. But the helicopter assembly line brought home to me quite forcibly that there was a built-in predisposition in what formerly had been an airplane assembly line to *resist the change* to helicopters and revert to airplane manufacture. This could be counteracted only by constant vigilance." (my italics)[29]

Turning inward is a step not to be skipped on the way to understanding your road, path, or open sea. There are compasses that point to the true north, towards a recognizable purpose. You can hold a compass in your hand, but there is also one in your heart. Navigation occurs with the blending of these two compasses. The most ultimate quest is one of orientation and devotion. If one doesn't attempt to know where one is going, in other words, to know one's evolution, then a built-in predisposition assumes the helm. Our habits resist the change that our spirits encourage and a vague feeling creeps in of being lost at sea.

Even with good navigation it is still likely for one to sometimes feel lost at sea. In these times it is best to turn to nature. Sit for even a moment under an apple tree. See its fruits and smell its smells. Become convinced of a world of spirit, where pies bring delight to little faces. As you recognize spirit externally you can remember once again who you really are and what you are capable of.

Just before we entered this spiral of existential questioning we were 'in love', or 'fascinated' with something or someone. The spiral of Venus and Saturn had us appropriately engaged. Keep in mind, time is of any scale. The toroscope reveals our capacity to metabolize time, that is to say, to 'draw time in and radiate time back out'. It is helpful just to look at the mirror image of the word 'time'; 'emit'. The taurus field generates an aura, and that aura is the time that we emit, or radiate back into the world after we have drawn it in.

Therefore the spiral of engagement that came before could be a fascinating piece of music or a lifelong commitment to another person. It could be a challenge so great that it consumes most of your time and powers of relating. Whatever form it takes, real engagement leads to existential questions. To become devoted to something calls for a real orientation and a consideration of 'what is possible.

To summarize the flow thus far: a spirited nature, Taurus, splits, or germinates with Gemini. It 'twins' with something and then re-experiences an idea of self, or nature. The various twinning strikes Virgo's bell which reverberates with biofeedback, at times coming more alive and animated, as a fuller nature awakens. With a fuller mind, Libran beauty presents itself as plentiful and all-surrounding. Something speaks most directly to you and you allow yourself to be drawn in, Saturnally contracted, maybe even committed.

And then once you find yourself in the most contracted place, a sudden Uranian awareness awakens you even further as you consider your future, and ask yourself how you want to further steer your focus, commitment or 'reality'. Only in the privacy of your inner life can you confront these most personal questions. And, often surprisingly, your intuitions *do* have an opinion, *a hunch*, a new light to shed on things. This is the power of the Moon; a light that comes from the depths and begins to grow.

In astrology, the Moon has to do with memory as well as the past and family. Inner light that begins to grow is memory at its most primal and creative. For it is the memory of who you are; a creative creature.

Similarly with family, the light of wisdom, warmth or spirit can continue for generations. Your intuitions, your hunches and glimmers of recognition are bound up with the warmth and wisdom of your ancestry. The flash of your great grandmother's smile is in your moonlit matrix. The past has real momentum, but most of us continue to steer without ample light because the light goes unrecognized. The autopilot that takes over knows nothing of examining the life worth living.

But if one can tune in and quiet down the confusion that surrounds by focusing and then foresighting (Saturn and Uranus) then a new light can be born.

As little kids my twin made a habit of singing to the Moon. I remember being in awe of how she could do this. It was like she had some secret understanding of lunar language. As adults this remains to be true. She plays the musical saw as well as other reverberating instruments like the mbira, piano and xylophone. Her compositions are like water, like Moonlight and the ocean itself. I once went through a year of feeling artistically uninspired and she sent me a book that she said would help; *Live Fast, Die Young: The Wild Ride of Making Rebel Without a Cause* by Al Weisel and Lawrence Frascella. Before I knew it I was delightfully obsessed with all things James Dean and Nick Ray. The rabbit hole was nourishingly deep and electric. I remember wondering *'how could I have been bored?'* I now understand this to be a return of moonlight, a renaissance of inner life. This sure feels good.

Inner life is what allows light to re-emerge and seek its union with the highest light, that is Sagittarius, or spiritedness. Jupiter, Sagittarius' planet, exalts in the lunar sign of Cancer. The light of hope, learning, and enthusiasm is born from within. It then can grow bigger than anything. If the light is truly born from within, the largeness will nourish and centralize you all the more with the cohesive power of love. As the poet William Blake said "No one soars too high if they soar with their own wings."

The purpose of understanding time-metabolism has the same goal as understanding it on a purely dietary one. We want to know how to get the most out of our nourishment. We want to know how to feed ourselves so that we can survive and thrive.

Because we are not separate from nature we also need to feed ourselves in a way that makes nature itself thrive. Big agriculture and an overly consumerist society has put heavy threats on the future of a flourishing nature. And as it is so often, the answer hides in the problem. An over consumerist society would do best to further understand what 'consuming' means. While 'consuming' means eating, drinking and buying, it also means something very simple: 'filling'.

You can fill your closet, your belly and your bank account but you can also fill your mind and your attention. You can fill your relationships with a committed and caring attitude. The chemical processes at play when you fill your mind and when you absorb yourself fully into something are potent! A passion that consumes can be powerful like a tornado. A mind consumed with solving a problem can save the lives of many and pave a brighter future for all.

Saturn, the planet of attention and focus, breaks down into roots *Sat* and *urn*, or 'satiated urn'. To fill up the urn is to saturate your focus, and make it likelier for your genius to find you. For Uranus, the sign of genius follows Saturn in the toroscope, as a wider awareness grows. And then when lightning strikes, a lodestone within knows true north. The moon is that rock inside that becomes magnetized by meaning. Its charge becomes a compass from within.

The Moon is slowly drifting away from the earth.[30] On a personal level we must chase her and try to keep her close. For she has the power. She has our power. We are free yet bound. Free to create, choose, and affirm yet bound to respond. Because we are not robotic, things affect us. It is precisely this affectivity that motivates us, as sure as the Moon raises the tides.

Spinoza said that all was cause and effect. He saw consciousness as something that sits between cause and effect. The best we can do is try and determine the true causes of effects, and thereby gain more control of our lives.[31]

More control is better navigation. That is ultimately what the Moon can help us with. If you can know what things affect you, how they affect you and then make rational choices accordingly you are tapping into toroidal strategy. A ballplayer recognizes that a wider batting stance ups his chances of getting a hit, so he employs it. An overworked nurse recognizes that a cluttered workstation makes her less patient with her patients so she makes a pledge to keep it neat. Developing an accurate vision of cause and effect can work wonders for your energy flow. The "I" that makes the change comes from your heroic fire, your eternal you. It bursts forth dramatically to save you from robotic tendency. As Camus said "With rebellion awareness is born."

The Age of Aquarius, or the renaissance of the water bearer, is a full embrace of lunar power; an ownership of our potencies to respond. Because we can determine true causes of effects, we can look creatively outward to shape experience that has shaped us.

With rebellion a new light has emerged from within. The light will begin to grow in the next spiral with Aries.

Acting

Aries and Scorpio

Chapter five

I can feel guilty about the past, apprehensive about the future, but only in the present can I act. Abraham Maslow

I don't have a favorite season, but I do recognize Springtime to have superhero qualities. It ushers forth in a most righteous act of defiance. Things get loud. Plants burst forth from gravel. People embrace a more natural and supple way of living. There is more smiling and strolling. Winter's rigidity is shaken off like a hearty laugh.

The spring is not only found all around it is found in your step! People spring into action with new plans and projects just as sure as the birds build their nests. Baby birds and squirrels are like ambassadors of springtime; we are born anew in their innocent scampers.

The glyph of Aries shows the triumph of a plant that pushes its way upward into the light of day. A time lapse motion of the plant reveals a whirly dance; the serpentine momentum of Scorpio. Each action of Aries builds into Scorpio momentum.

Like the upward push of the plant, time moves in a distinct direction: forward. It doesn't go backward. Anyone who has missed a train knows this to be true.

But what about the *forwardness* of the train? Its mighty engine that delights the spirits of young children? Is this the same forwardness of the clock that sometimes can't move fast enough from the doldrums of a cubicle at 3:15? Is the tick-tock forward the same forward as the plant that pushes its way into living?

It isn't the same because the tick-tock of a clock is mechanical and the forward push of a plant is biological, or natural, not to mention heroic. A heartbeat that matches the tick-tock of a clock is not as healthy as a heartbeat with consistent variability. Heart rate variability, or *HVR*[32], is the measure of a healthy heartbeat which is consistent but not mechanical. The same could be said of good character. Good character is consistent but not mechanical.

Leap seconds are added to the world clock to compensate for the earth's slowing rotation. There are no straight lines in nature. There is no tick-tock in the real world of wholeness. We employ tick-tock to gain more control.

Circadian rhythms reveal a time that exists within our biochemistry. French Astronomer Jean Jacques d'"Ortous de Mairan discovered this when he put a mimosa plant in a dark room back in 1729. The mimosa plant continued to unfold its leaves in the morning and fold them at night. Somehow the plant 'knew' when it was time to sleep and time to awaken. Any jetlagged passenger can relate.

Aging advances the biological clock. Yet there are seventy year olds whose body tissues are 'younger' than other seventy year olds. Doctor Greg Fahy designed and led the TRIIM trial[33] which published the first report of thymus regeneration in a normal human. Amazingly, his subjects seemed to "age in reverse". His method is to "regenerate the thymus gland" by administering a "growth hormone cocktail" to his patients at steady intervals. The result showed a reverse of the biological clock.

The thymus gland is a most mysterious thing. In the springtime of our youth it is large and growing larger. But when bodies stop growing the thymus begins to shrink. Past the age of sixty it is mostly gone, replaced by fatty tissue. Yet this gland is said to be the masters of our immunity. How we hate to see it go!

Gorillas pound the thymus gland to assert their alpha dominance. Athletes often pound the 'high heart' after hitting a homerun or scoring a goal. Roman soldiers would rub the herb 'thyme' on their chests before going to battle. Could it be that time's biological 'forward push' is found in the integrity of the thymus gland?

Where do we point when we say the word "me"? To the high heart, the thymus gland. Could the biological forward push be our most natural identities, centered on indestructible spirit?

Thymos is a Greek word for "spiritedness" as well as "honor and self-recognition". Greek myths and great works of literature like the Odyssey explore the characters' relationship to their thymos as they strive to keep intact their own spirited honor with as much truth and honesty as their souls can discern. Complex moral scenarios drive the plot and the challenging evolution of their spirits.

The forward push of time calls to its creator for transcendence. We created time not to be ruled by it but to help us rule our own lives. There is never enough time in the day. Time is money. Time is ruthless and unforgiving. But you *are* time in the form of spirited thymos. You are time as your thymos sings its way forward by growing, learning and becoming.

You are time with every springtime, every novelty that finds its way to you and makes you feel young at heart. The challenge is to know this kind of time to be as real as the clock's tick-tock. For the truth is that it is *more real*. Thymos is a time beyond time.

Mars, and Aries is the first blast of fire in the toroscope. Fire is action and light. Arthur M. Young explains that "*Light is pure action*, unattached to any object, like the smile without the cat" (his italics).[34] He goes on further to say that light exists outside of time because it is non physical, that is to say that it is without mass. "For the photon, a pulse of light, *time does not exist; clocks stop at the speed of light*." (his italics)

The evergreen herb, thyme, that was rubbed on the soldiers chests carried an eternal signature of life pushing forward, in other words evolution. Pierre Teilhard de Chardin said "evolution marches uphill."[35] Heroes are compelling characters in books and movies because they don't lose order in time. They make something good out of their circumstances with decisive action. Decisive characters are impelling and worth our time as watchers! Time is worthy when time is thymos. We are far more in touch with our own worthiness when we are thymos and recognize ourselves to be spirited in our own forward push, our own eternal spring.

The forward push is up for ownership. Will it be owned by the machine? The metronome without a soul that looms large? Or will it be owned by you as thymos, an affirmation of your own evolution, a celebration of your own spirit, a readiness to behold something new?

The momentum of a moving train is cinematic, purposeful and triumphant in the eyes of the child. They have not yet learned to simply see it as a cue to pick up your bags and head to the platform. The song of action sings like springtime birds and affirms the reality of the spirit.

What about your own momentum? Do you feel it to be powerful or purposeful? Is it a runaway train? Is it a buildup of reactive subconscious actions? A chug chug of frustration from actions that go thwarted? Is it collecting dust deep in the station with a belief that nothing is worth doing?

The first book that Dolly Parton's Reading Library book sent to our house was the Little Engine That Could. It is not a quick book for a two year old, but my son would get drawn into the story every time. He would stay awake until the end with eyes growing larger. "I think I can, I think I can" would inspire an ear to ear smile every time. We read that book so often that it was scotch taped in various places. I had taped the pages in the wrong order at one point but quickly got used to the detour route before taking the time to retape them. This book was so real to him. This kind of forwardness was so real and understood. But even now as he is about to turn four, the forwardness of time deeply eludes. He often asks "what did we do tomorrow when I was a tiny baby?"

The North American Railway adopted a standardized way of keeping time in 1883. This finally made it possible for one to arrive somewhere at the "right time."

Imagine having no concept of the right time. Cell phones bring time's margin of error down all the more. The tick-tock world is gaining strength. 6:00 a.m. means 6:00 a.m. Everyone knows if you are indeed 5 minutes late.

But what about another kind of "right time". The one that smiles with the rising sun, in the words of Bob Marley, as your circadian rhythm locks into the rhythm of the day? What about the right times in your life where you knew you had to do something right then, or risk watching a train pass you by?

With a clock, you pinpoint a right time that will cycle back again twelve hours later. It's not so with momentum. Momentum, like true time, only moves forward. A question of "rightness" when it comes to momentum can only refer to a "right direction". There is only one "right direction" in the business of living: *forward*. Evolution marches uphill.

Clocks and calendars are tools. We connect to their meanings and use them to gain more control. Though we can control showing up to a train on time, we can't control time itself. Unless it is *our own "time"*; *our own momentum*. Personal momentum is the only kind of time we can control. To be in better and better control of our own momentum is what we are after.

Momentum swirls beneath the surface of everyone you meet. There are lifetimes of information stored within these 'powerhouses', largely forgotten but never lost. Momentum guides us all, half asleep.

Times' arrow moves forward. But does your momentum support your decisive forwardness, your thymos? Is your momentum building power to your chosen center of gravity (the Moon)? Or is it working against it?

You are not a passive bystander watching the wheel turn round and round. Rather, you are an action hero. You don't just show up on time for the train, *you are the train*. You are an engine of triumph that inspires delight to those who see it.

Colin Wilson says that passivity renders the world less real because when someone sinks into long-term passivity and discouragement "the vital batteries go flat and everything becomes meaningless and joyless."[36] In short, passivity makes a person *forget to steer the wheel.* They forget to relate to what they encounter from a productive orientation. Many trains of possibility pass by because the traveler made no room for them to be seen. There was no readiness, no hope to encounter the 'real yet unborn'.

The toroscope displays the Moon spiraling into Mars, the planet of action. In nature, the Moon inspires a lot of action. The tides rise and fall. Scorpions glow underground, cities of sea creatures come alive with bioluminescent celebration. Corals go into a mass spawning, birds synchronize their flights. The Moon, with all of its privacy and charge of feeling, can move mountains of activity.

Likewise, your Moon, your 'chosen center of gravity' is *what should inspire action in your life.* Actions that support the flourishing of your unique nature will strengthen the flow and make your energy field more robust. No one would argue the logic of this when it comes to a home cooked meal and a good night's sleep. But once the basic needs are met there are many more actions that your fertile nature churns and yearns to take. These are not as easily recognized as rational;, but we can train ourselves to see them as so.

The teacher that orients herself to inspire a love of learning will likely be more patient with 'silly' questions. A piano player that orients himself to express the magnificence of the high heavens will likely put in more than an hour a day of practice. The orientation takes into account one's most private feelings. The inwardness turns outward again when we take action. As Colin Wilson says "It is not just a question of turning inward, it is turning inward to come to terms with interior problems and then turning outward again."[37]

Feeling is what motivates (Cancer to Aries). Actions then shape momentum, or power (Aries to Scorpio). The Moon is a force that mysteriously pulls. It pulls forth the tides and beckons the birds to make them more raucous. It draws the racoon out of his home and the howl out of the wolf. What does it pull in you?

Have you ever ordered Chinese just because you were in the mood? Have you ever 'felt like' taking a bike ride or getting dressed up or playing Wordle? Moods shapeshift like the Moon. The shapeshifting mood shapeshifts behavior which shapeshifts our lives! If one has no command over their ship, no center of gravity from which to navigate, then power is given away. Moods take over like fast moving rain clouds. There is far less order and far more likeliness of getting stuck in deadening habits.

With a burst of fire, Mars celebrates what the toroscope is based on: freedom. You are free to know your true causes. You are free to know your true callings, your true feelings. Most importantly, you are free to act in accordance with your true nature, and therefore free to truly come to know yourself. You are free to create real and authentic bounty. This is how one builds power and toroidal strength.

Aries' Ram is not simply a headstrong creature who butts his horns. The horns actually show an important pattern; that is, the indrawing spiral. Wide at the periphery, they draw smaller towards the center. This represents the indrawing nature of subjectivity. Subjectivity does not arise out of nowhere. The wider world is drawn into a private center. From the private center, represented by the Moon, a new light is born. The Ram identifies with the new light. Because this identity is rooted in real inner light, actions become natural. The tightrope walker learns to balance. The poet learns to listen.

Once again, time scales are irrelevant for the torus field. One's lunar navigation can shift in an instant and establish a new orientation from which to act. Just watch a good actor at work. Their inner life changes in response to a charged up scene and their actions shift accordingly.

Actions begin the trinity of fire in the toroscope. The fire rises up and up to the upper air rich with nitrogen, the very element that can induce laughter in the human body. Fire goes all the way up. Freedom is the nature of light and action, existing beyond the laws of time. It is a time of a different kind. Not tick-tock time but *pure potential*; a time based on freedom. With a blast of independence we come to know ourselves as thymos, a spirited biological time, a potency to take action.

The philosopher Friedrich Wilhelm Joseph Schelling said "Time is not something that flows independently of the self; *the self itself* is time conceived of in activity."[38]

To feel the bliss of inner freedom is to align your actions with your inner light so that your life takes on meaning. Because that is ultimately what fire rises for.

Consider the "time conceived of in activity" when a basketball player makes the winning basket with seconds left on the clock at a home game finals. How about the "time" conceived of in activity when standing up for someone you love, or building a log cabin, or baking a perfect pie from some leisurely picked apples on a sunny autumn afternoon.

There is no "time" divorced from activity. Passivity renders the world less real because reality (time) is bound up with our inner freedom, which is to say, our propensity to act and make those actions count.

Affirming

Leo and Pisces

Chapter six

What is eternity? It is the sun mixed with the sea. Arthur Rimbaud

What a treat it is to gaze upon the sun mixed with the sea. The dancing light skims the magnitude of the sea as two unfathomable worlds collide. It becomes hard not to dream, not to affirm all of your surroundings wholeheartedly. Without realizing it, we join its eternity.

The fleeting sparkle spells a limerick-like truth; that eternity can only be glimpsed, or briefly tasted. But such an encounter can be treasured as eternity's proof, or *knowledge of eternity.* One can come to rely on an inner sun that affirms the places where eternity is glimpsed; well-lit places of joy, learning, love and delight. Eternity lives in the instant, in the life of the light. We can't hold on to it but we can share its eternity with our delight, and our light of understanding of its meaning. As the poet William Blake said "he who binds himself to a joy does the winged life destroy. But he who kisses it as it flies lives in eternity's sunrise".

The Sun and Neptune bring in the wisdom of poets, those who can perceive a wholeness through an artistic synthesis of what they see.

We begin as poets. Children have no problem affirming the delights of what they see, and employing their imaginations to extend the scenery ever farther. Magnitude is assumed with children, the mundane is abstract. They happily kiss the joy as it flies and they look forward to the joys that will come next.

The sea builds a saltwater synapse of memory. The more eternity that is kissed the more magical the sea. Enchantment becomes a subconscious mode of being. Children live in a more subconscious mode than adults with their predominance of delta and theta brainwaves. These brain waves are slower moving, more relaxed and restorative. They begin to speed up as we get older and the cinematic enchantment of childhood shifts into the adult perspective of 'real time'. We enter into the mode of dealing with external events.

But the magic need not be abandoned. For magic is just productivity. As we grow we gain the rewards of being able to do things in the world like grown ups can. We learn to walk safely down the road, and tie our shoes and get dressed. We learn how to balance on a bike without falling by playing with our centers of gravity. We begin to master the laws that were always befuddling us. As we grow into adults, we have mastered many laws. But have we remembered to *make the turn*? Have we remembered to turn towards the light; of joy, meaning and affirmation?

True affirmation can only come from a true place. Children affirm naturally because spontaneous joy is how they are wired to learn. Learning and playing go hand in hand. Children must play to learn. They naturally turn to the light, of delight, of learning, of playing. Just imagine learning your abc's without first singing it.

Natural light is always within reach. Relating to light wholeheartedly is like dancing in the full spectrum of the sun. It is like the athlete affirming the fullness of his potential in an instant, or the artist bringing coherence to her creation. Relating wholeheartedly brings a deep sense of peace, as sure as a genuine laugh eases social tension. How can we cultivate this?

A lizard who has grown lethargic bathes in the sun. The rays of the sun *reanimate* him and he continues on with his business. He knows instinctively to seek out warmth that comes with a full-spectrum of color. He can depend on its 'charge'.

My mom is a triple Leo (Sun, Moon and Mercury). Her warmth, like the Sun, is a charge so constant that I and many of her lucky friends can always count on it. One time I was on a crowded train looking for a seat. I kindly asked a business woman if I could sit where her legs were stretched out as she read the paper. She gave me a most irritated look and huffed as she sat up straight, fixing her eyes crossly back on her reading material. The iciness was so unnatural. As I sat beside her negative aura, an image flashed through my mind. It was an image of how my mom would have responded to the same request from a stranger in search of a seat. She would have bounced up as if to say "oops!". Then she would have tossed in a warm smile with little half-moon squinty eyes. I sat there feeling so honored to have been raised by someone so wise, so natural.

In the body, the Sun, or Leo rules the heart. As reflective thinkers, the warmth of the sun can be 'tried on for size' so to speak. What warms one heart can familiarize one with their inner sun. And just like the lizard (or me with my mom!), one can come to depend on its charge.

The heart doesn't just warm with the sentimental, it also warms with holding wisdom and embracing vibrance. At its most basic signature, the Sun affirms life. T.S. Elliot wrote "where is the life we've lost in the living?".[39] The Sun that comes out from the clouds on a chilly day reminds one that "living" can be heightened, brightened, warmed and re-charged.

Did you ever find yourself on a kind of dead-end street simply because "your heart wasn't in it"? Leo's heart brings coherence to our lives. It synthesizes meaning with your unique set of dreams and hopes. It seeks to unify not fragment. It needs big picture visions not trivial facts. It needs purpose not "shoulds and shouldn'ts".

The sun is the heart's open embrace. Its vulnerability is its strength. A calloused heart can't love as fully as one that's been tenderized.

Without the unifying fire of love and purpose then the burst of Aries' thymos (the "time" conceived of in activity) would be nothing more than a firecracker at night. The slow burn of purpose and dreams sustains the spark and carries it onward to something greater.

Pisces is the last sign of the zodiac. It has accumulated all of the zodiac's traits, and it expresses it as a deep and sublime sense of peace. The serene wash of the cricket meadow is the unity of all activity. It is the ongoing promptings of the subconscious mind; one's trance and connection to the all. Pisces is the frontier of the productive imagination, where your own ideals and dreams are as worth your time as story books are to children.

Spinoza defined joy and sorrow in very simple terms. He said that joy was the passage from a less perfect condition to a more perfect one and that sorrow was the opposite.

The spiral of Moon and Uranus allows us to "drop in and see what condition our condition is in" to paraphrase the great Kenny Rogers. The change leads to an action, which is the next spiral of Mars and Pluto. Hunger leads us to eat food. The spiral of Sun and Neptune wants to *affirm this action with all of our being*. If we reached for a perfect and balanced lunch and ate it in the park with friends in sunshine, one might imagine the full near spiritual affirmation of Sun and Neptune. Disney movies dramatize these kinds of peak experiences by making all of the fish and birds sing in a unified and spirited world. Yet this world is real. People do at times feel that they are walking on sunshine. Van Gogh painted the world ablaze with beauty and meaning. It has to do with affirming your thymos, or spiritedness, in the real world in which time passes. It is about the recognition of light, within you and around you. Scrooge singing Merry Christmas out his window is the age old tale of recognizing the light. One grows large with magnitude and spirituality. The interrelatedness of all things is recognized. Your magnitude is the magnitude of the sun and the sea. Joy and connectedness expands one's being.

The French have a word; 'profiter' which translates as 'to profit'. It is a casual term that they use often. One can profit off of a nice walk, or a delicious meal, or sitting outside in the sun. It's like a reminder to really enjoy what you are doing. Everyone can begin to feel rich if they remember to profit often enough. It is easily forgotten that all of our economy traces back to the values of gold, the authentic luster of the sun. Joy is free and it will make you rich. If you soak up enough profit, or existential sunshine, your memory bank becomes rich too. Neptune, or the sea within, carries this wealth through your body. Your imagination and daydreaming begin to support more discoveries of gold, meaning, or joy. Joseph Campbell said if you "follow your bliss doors will open where there weren't any doors before".

The spirit of play is conducive to learning. Finesse is the result of having learned something so well that it becomes expressed effortlessly. A spotlight on a figure skater is the sun mixed with the sea. She has learned her skill so deeply that she can express, or radiate it like the sun. Her full body memory is like the ocean, what the Egyptians called "mem". The light has been so deeply absorbed into the salty matrix of memory that it can now radiate back out, under full conscious control.

Learning is another version of sunbathing, profiting or collecting gold. The light of meaning is golden, adhering to the highest of standards. False meaning is as useless as false gold. It can't be stored, absorbed and embraced like true meaning. If it is then it will only be shattered as a house of cards on which one tried to build. For real sturdiness you need real meaning, just as a plant needs real sunlight.

At its most basic definition, light is something that *makes vision possible*. But vision extends way beyond a set of eyes. Imagination allows for innervisions whose source of light comes from within. Vision brings a sense of unity to action, holding a worthy future in its field. Vision animates and inspires. It affirms adventure and agency. A healthy vision can connect us with our purpose. An affinity for light can keep us animated, like the lizard with its rock.

Ultimately what we are arriving at in this outer spiral of sun and sea is a cohesive affirmation of living, and all that makes living more lively. The heights and depths of the sun and the sea speak to the heights and depths of love itself. To love is to be vulnerable, and feel what others feel. It is to celebrate the shared joys of experience as well as share the pain of sorrows.

Love is unifying, it brings people together. Love for a vision brings a single person together with themselves, with a sense of purpose and integrity. As we move outward in our torus field we stumble evermore upon the centrifugal force of love, or what Pierre Teilhard de Chardin called "radial energy". He said "union is fuller being...union increases only through an increase in consciousness, that is to say vision. And that, doubtless, is why the history of the living world can be summarized as the elaboration of ever more perfect eyes within a cosmos in which there is always something more to be seen."[40]

The Sun and the sea expands our energy field higher and deeper, brighter and vaster. The warmth of love is also the brightness of vision. Moment to moment there is also always something more to be seen. The trouble is we have blinders. Some of the blinders are necessary ones, keeping us from a constant bombardment of the senses, but other blinders are more pesky. People can stumble into the horrible habit of over-familiarizing things and taking too much for granted.

When this happens a trance takes over, not the waltz-like trance of childhood, but the metronome theme of robots and insects. The Moon failed to offer fresh light, and the assumptions of the past are all that guide us. Aries' action is no longer the springtime of triumph but rather the marching of ants. Pluto casts the robotic trance. Eternity has been injured. Vision has lost its luster and distance. There is no readiness to behold something new and be moved by it. We begin to rigidify like the tinman, convinced he has no heart.

But the solar creature is the cat and cats stay supple. Their spontaneous reactions to feathers may be hilarious but they also point to something sacred: a readiness to jump in on the fun and grapple with the strange.

A dog's sense of fun is more bound up with lunar themes. The familiarity of a favorite ball delights the dog. He can learn tricks because he delights in the powers of the Moon to reflect the sun, that is to say the powers of memory to express what was learned.

Neptune, the sea, shows water's deepest expressions of memory. The dog astounds and the game seems to play him. His actions are so fluid, so graceful with finesse.

But not the cat. He slams against the wall with the introduction of a sparkly toy. He is so ready to be moved. Though he may smooth back his ears after falling off the couch, we all know that he had a moment of bliss/chaos with respect to something new.

And this is an important quality. This is why laughs can take over and even destroy a job interview. Dancing can make one lose all sense of time.

Philosopher Henri Bergson saw laughter to be an evolutionary strategy to protect us from too much rigidity. He said that in general we "laugh at something mechanical encrusted upon the living". The classic gag of someone slipping on a banana peel can demonstrate. Someone is moving along fluidly and then a silly banana peel renders them bumbling and stumbling like a broken down lawn mower. The mechanical has encrusted itself on the living, and our souls know to laugh.

Above the sun god Apollo's temple of Delphi read the words "know thyself". If one is to radiate a sense of confidence, like a sun emitting rays of light, then it must come from an authentic place. Otherwise the confidence is unstable, and likely overcompensating for such instability. This may produce a pompous type, a know-it-all, a person who likes to make others feel small so they can seem big by comparison. But how does one come to truly "know oneself?" Could this be a question of continuous navigation, affirmed in the heights of one's heart?

Take an example of a school bus driver who has navigated the neighborhood roads for years. Not only this, he has also navigated his own conduct as a positive role model for the kids, and is known for his good character. All of this navigating has built up power. His sense of self is bound up with this power. His actions come from a center of gravity, a pledge he has made to drive the kids safely and also be a nice presence in their lives. There is so much coherence with his actions to his pledge, his lunar centering (turning the corners, greeting the kids) that he becomes graceful. With an ocean of subconscious activity *supporting* his actions instead of fighting them, he exudes a zen-like peace. His smile and laugh are genuine because his solar heart has stayed supple and ready for life to surprise him.

It is too often that our oceans *do not* support our actions. The biggest reason for this is a *lack of orientation*. If one does not choose a center of gravity that choice will be constantly made for them by their reactions to things, thoughts, other people and scenery. When your reactions are all that make your lodestone, then your north star is nowhere. You are out at sea without any guidance.

Perhaps more important than this though is that there is *no starting point for your power to grow*. There is no cinema in your life. No romance. No meaning. Life is a series of reactions to this and that and the fragmented world is what's 'real'. But this is a lie. The more coherence you can integrate into your life the more real your world. Because your world includes the reality of the spirit. And it is the spirit's aim to unify not divide.

The Nature of Spirit

Sagittarius

Chapter seven

The highest activity a human being can attain is learning for
understanding, because to understand is to be free. Baruch Spinoza

I was not raised with any religion. The closest that religion came to my family was on my mother's side with Quaker meetings. I have a vague memory of attending one of the meetings and wondering who would start speaking. I didn't understand anything about it but I did understand that it was somehow important.

George Fox started the Quaker movement in 1652 by encouraging his followers to look to their inner light for guidance rather than that of the church. He was arrested and jailed several times for his beliefs.

Walt Whitman, who was raised with Quaker principles wrote "George Fox stands for something too- a thought- the thought that wakes in silent hours- perhaps the deepest, most eternal thought latent in the human soul. This is the thought of God, merged in the thoughts of moral right and the immortality of identity. Great, great is this thought- aye, greater than all else."[41]

I have no religion, but like many others who don't attend a church I have a strong connection to something 'greater than all else'.

I can feel it beneath my feet in the grass. I can see it in the midst of a happy moment. I can sense it in the integrity of someone else. I can know it in my most memorable joys. It is very real.

Mark Twain said "Man is a Religious Animal".[42] There is a solid kernel of truth to our human design that defies scientific proving. Science allows us to measure many things but it can't measure *everything*. In fact it can't measure a lot of things! It can measure the ratios of shapes in a butterfly's wing but it can't measure its beauty. It can measure the distance from earth to a certain star yet it can't measure its magnitude.

Yet magnitude exists, beauty exists, around you and within you. The poet Gaston Bachelard writes "Immensity is within ourselves. It is attached to a sort of expansion of being that life curbs and caution arrests, but which starts again when we are alone."[43]

Sagittarius' planet, Jupiter, is the same sign of Saturn, just flipped. There is a mirror image of something important at play. Saturn is known for its efforts, its integrity, its solitude and its maturity. Jupiter is known for its hope, its spirit, its beliefs and its learning. But are these not two sides of the same coin?

Effort without hope is useless. It brings to mind the sad parable of Sysyphus pushing the rock uphill for all eternity. Integrity without belief is impossible. One must know what they believe in order to collect oneself and have a perspective on things. Maturity without learning doesn't happen, no matter what.

Saturn represents chronological time. Cronos, in Greek mythology, was forewarned that one of his children would succeed him so he began to eat them. At last his wife Rhea decided to put an end to this and swaddled a stone instead of her latest born. Cronos ate the stone and the baby Zeus was spared. He grew up to force Cronos to disgorge his brothers and sisters and he defeated him in war.

Jupiter was the Roman name for Zeus, the god of quaking thunder and the sky. Balancing out Saturn's laws of time is Jupiter's quaking freedom and spirit. For law and freedom are two sides of the same coin, as are certainty and uncertainty.

Heisenberg's Uncertainty Principle eradicated certainty from the measurable world in 1927, but that is not to say that certainty doesn't exist. For there is *another world* of which we are a part;

an immeasurable world. A world of qualities not quantities. A world of beauty, meaning, zest, magnitude, art and hope.

To the extent that Saturn reveals a solid and scientific ground to stand on Jupiter reveals the 'wind beneath our wings' and the sunshine that we walk upon. If we can measure something to the n'th degree and become masters of precision, can we not also aspire to become masters of spirit and allow spiritedness to further our flourishing?

Jupiter and Saturn represent the age-old debate between free-will and determinism. Which one is real? Are we free or fated? The toroscope reveals an intimate partnership between fate and free-will. For the glyph is simply flipped, fate and free-will are but reversed expressions of the same thing. Arthur M. Young called determinism "the agency of free-will".[44] He gives the example of starting your keys in the car. If it weren't for determinism or law, then you could never count on the car to start. You may be free to decide to drive to California but that is nothing if you can't use determined means (i.e the car that starts) to get there.

Colin Wilson called freedom "release from unreality".[45] He said "it is as impossible to exercise freedom in an unreal world as it is to jump while falling".[46]

Light dove into matter the day you took your first breath. The upper air of the Gods took root in you and a very special churning process began. Your birth chart is a reflection of you emancipating from nature's unity, or as Jung called it the 'unus mundus'. The question for every birth chart is this: *what did you become free for?*

The nature of spirit is a feeling of inner freedom. But it isn't freedom from anything, it is freedom *for* something. It is the origin of all; a freedom that is already owned and assumed. It connects to Taurus, or the center of nature, to creatively animate one's 'field'. This is why Sagittarius is the *centaur*. The true center of the Taurus field (cenTAUR) is the spirited magnitude that stretches beyond all measure, in other words, the feeling of inner freedom. Freedom dives into matter so that it can *do something with its freedom.* The 'smile without the cat' yearns for the cat! Freedom is nothing without a means to express and exercise that freedom, that is to say, without the laws and limits of the natural world.

Arthur Eddington theorized that the curve of space time and the curve of uncertainty that exists within each photon were really the same thing. He called this 'the phase dimension'. In this dimension there is no time, only rotation. Arthur M. Young saw this dimension to be the same as 'choice', a freedom always present in some capacity.[47]

Unlike the zodiac wheel which is based on the turning of time and law, the torus field rotates and centers itself on freedom. Your choices have the power to strengthen or weaken the field.

When I say that the nature of spirit is a feeling of inner freedom, you may find yourself wondering; just a feeling? Is that to say that spirit isn't real?

To this question let's ask another: is consciousness real? Are your experiences real? Ultimately all experiences are 'feeling experiences', and consciousness is really 'the feeling of being conscious'.

The feeling of inner freedom is real; it is the spirited fire that infuses all of nature. Abraham Maslow's study of the characteristics of healthy people revealed a tendency for them to have 'peak experiences',[48] or moments of sheer affirmation in which all of life seemed to take on more meaning.

What is really happening is a *building of light*. It starts with the Moon, when a subjective centering is embraced. The navigating that ensues based on this centering is a chain of actions and the inner light continues to build on itself (the Aries

Scorpio spiral). At last a stable sense of self is affirmed and supported by one's deep subconscious wiring as the Sun-Neptune spiral shows. From here there is quite simply a lot of potential for overflow; of joy, meaning, and zest, represented by Sagittarius.

Colin Wilson was right when he suspected that the peak experience can be induced at will. Maslow was convinced this was impossible. The toroscope reveals a suitable map towards an increase of peak experience. This is not to say that it is easy. Remember that the moon's inner light reveals itself in response to that which we deem worthy of our time and effort. It is only when we focus ourselves into something else that our awareness grows large and our moonlight flickers from within. Our natures are full of knowledge as is the nature that surrounds us. The flow of the torus is a steady intake of the world so that we can radiate ourselves back into the world and create alongside nature.

Nature is spirited. The nature of spirit is to rise and go higher, like fire. The nature of spirit is to aspire and grow not only in size but in coherence.

When our spirits grow and our lives take on more knowledge and meaning, all of this fire dives back into our natures (Taurus) creating a fuller capacity to establish ever more *real relations.* We make our natures sturdier, more robust as our spirits grow.

It is a process. It starts from a sense of self that reaches out into the world and retrieves information. This is shown by Taurus that sits in the middle of mind, the Mercuries, and gives an elegant design of consciousness. But spirit presupposes the self. What is funny is that we may go our whole lives never knowing this, or feeling this to be true. Yet it is true. If we can manage to be curious enough about things and others so that our minds can become fuller and more animated then we begin a path. If we can come to engage with our surroundings appropriately, and focus ourselves into the places that truly 'speak' to us, we may awaken. Our awareness may widen and our inner life may deepen. Then comes a light. Our own light. What will become of it?

Will we embrace the meaning that awakened within and further center ourselves. Will we embrace an authentic 'ego' as a captain embraces his ship? Will our actions support this sense of 'recognition'? Can we build more and more power and come to radiate our true selves with grace and fluidity? Will we attain a birds eye view of our life and see big picture meaning in the mundane? Will spirit, or the inner light that we have grown, merge with the spirit of the upper air in a burst of peak experience. For really there is no division between the two. Your light inside is magnificent, and all surrounding, especially when you help foster its growth.

The unity of birds in flight is spirit in action. For spirit is action at its highest and most uniting. A glimmer of recognition can point to what you became free for. Your memory knows. Your ancestry has a part in it. Most of all, your potency to respond and be affected deserves your dedicated attention.

As a baby, your umbilical cord kept you alive by indrawing the 'sea' of your mother's blood and nutrients. At birth, the cord is cut. Your navel, bearing the same shape of Cancer's whirlpool, continues to draw in a 'sea'. But it is a different sea; a sea of feeling. This is what butterflies in the stomach really are. Perhaps it is why the word navel and navigate are similar. You used to *not* be the captain of your own ship. Ever since birth you have been slowly perfecting the skill of navigation, with a most precious 'birthmark' to remind you.

No one can peer into your inner life and see the light that you recognize. It is only by your consistent action that you can express such light and only then can others see it. When it is truly authentic it is recognized by others just as you recognized it in yourself. Authenticity has a luster, like gold, like the aurum of a healthy aura.

The nature of spirit is inner freedom, and inner freedom is rooted in the potential for you to recognize your inner light and share it with others.

Recognizing the light is the nature of spirit, be it the light within or the light in others and in nature. Your recognition of light outside of you also births your own light from within.

This is how freedom is bound. Inner freedom draws from substance, it is not manifested out of thin air. To be truly free means to *feel* it. And you can't feel it if it isn't there. The spiritedness that you feel through your choices and actions is how you truly come to know yourself.

In closing, what I wish for you to take from this book is an invitation. I invite you to explore the mechanics of your human design with this ancient map. You can begin anywhere and jump around to different signs and archetypes. I invite you to play with your powers of mind; see how something interesting wakes up your full mind and sends forth fresh energy. Play with your powers of engagement, and see how your focus and commitment can foster the real growth of bounty and beauty. Play with your ideas of the future and find a suitable center of gravity from which to navigate. Play with your ability to take action from your center of gravity and see what swirls of power you can create. Play with your powers to affirm your progress and let your sun shine bright and your seas dream even bigger. And at last, play with spirit. Play with the surplus of light, the overflow of well-being, the 'greatest of all' substance that underlies all existence. Practice recognizing light in yourself, others and nature. Be ready to feel that inner freedom. Come to know it as yourself. If you can play with these themes then you are well on your way to mastering your torus flow. I wish you all the best with your discoveries!

With love,

Tess Hadley Durand

Works Cited

"The Art of Stress-Free Productivity: David Allen at TEDxClaremontColleges." *YouTube*, 31 October 2012,

Bachelard, Gaston. *The Poetics of Space*. Translated by Maria Jolas, Penguin Publishing Group, 2014.

Barfield, Owen. *Saving the Appearances: A Study in Idolatry*. Wesleyan University Press, 1988.

Brooks, Gwendolyn. *The Essential Gwendolyn Brooks: (American Poets Project #19)*. Library of America, 2005.

Brown, Margaret Wise. *My World Lap Edition*. HarperCollins, 2008.

Csikszentmihalyi, Mihaly. *Flow: The Psychology of Optimal Experience*. HarperCollins, 2008.

Damasio, Antonio. "The Evolving Minds Of Humans." *NPR*, 12 November 2010,

Damasio, Antonio R. *The Feeling of what Happens: Body and Emotion in the Making of Consciousness*. Harcourt Brace, 1999.

Eicher, David. "Ask Astro: How quickly is the Moon moving away from Earth?" *Astronomy Magazine*, 23 August 2022,

Einstein, Albert. "Albert Einstein, Course Author | AMNH." *American Museum of Natural History*,

Einstein, Albert. *The Ultimate Quotable Einstein.* Edited by Alice Calaprice, Princeton University Press, 2010.

Emerson, Ralph Waldo. *Essays and Lectures.* Library of America, 1983.

Fromm, Erich. *Man for Himself: An Inquiry Into the Psychology of Ethics.* Henry Holt and Company, 1990.

Fromm, Erich. *To have or to be?* Edited by Ruth Nanda Anshen, Harper & Row, 1976.

"Heart rate variability: How it might indicate well-being." *Harvard Health*, 22 November 2017,

Howell, Alice O., and Sylvia Perera. *Jungian Symbolism in Astrology: Letters from an Astrologer.* Theosophical Publishing House, 1987.

James, William. *The Varieties of Religious Experience.* Random House Publishing Group, 1999.

"Losing Paradise." *YouTube*, 29 October 2012, https://www.youtube.com/watch?v=fWTd-jwUOjU&ab_channel=SimonBrighton.

Maslow, Abraham H. *Toward a psychology of being.* Wiley, 1999.

Pieper, Josef. *Leisure: The Basis of Culture ; The Philosophical Act.* Ignatius Press, 2009.

Schelling, F. WJ. *System des trancendentalen Idealismus.* Gesammelte Schriften, 1794-1800.

Seifer, Marc. *Wizard: The Life and Times of Nikola Tesla.* Citadel Press, 2011.

Spinoza, Benedictus de. *The Ethics and Selected Letters.* Edited by Seymour Feldman, translated by Samuel Shirley, Hackett Publishing Company, 1982.

Stanley, Colin, and Colin Wilson. *Super Consciousness: The Quest for the Peak Experience.* Watkins Media, 2019.

Teilhard de Chardin, Pierre. *The Phenomenon of Man.* HarperCollins, 2008.

Vitale, Tom. "Billie Holiday: Emotional Power Through Song." *NPR*, 22 November 2010,

Wilson, Colin. *The Age of Defeat.* Edited by Samantha Devin, Aristeia Press, 2018.

Wilson, Colin. *Introduction to The New Existentialism.* Edited by Samantha Devin, Aristeia Press, 2019.

Wilson, Colin. *The Outsider.* Pan Books, 1978.

Wilson, Colin. *Religion and the Rebel.* Edited by Samantha Devin, Aristeia Press, 2017.

Young, Arthur M. *The Reflexive Universe: Evolution of Consciousness.* Anodos Foundation, 199

Endnotes

1. Brown, Margaret Wise. *My World Lap Edition*. HarperCollins, 2008. p1-2

2. Damasio, Antonio. "The Evolving Minds Of Humans." *NPR*, 12 November 2010, https://www.npr.org/2010/11/12/131274187/the-evolving-minds-of-humans.

3. Young, Arthur M. *The Reflexive Universe: Evolution of Consciousness pp. 262-267*

4. Seifer, Marc. *Wizard: The Life and Times of Nikola Tesla*. Citadel Press, 2011. p.25

5. Einstein, Albert. "Albert Einstein, Course Author | AMNH." *American Museum of Natural History*, p.325

6. Spinoza, Benedictus de. *The Ethics and Selected Letters*. p.43

7. Barfield, Owen. *Saving the Appearances: A Study in Idolatry*. Wesleyan University Press, 1988. p.42

8. *E. E. Cummings (1998). "No Thanks", p.58, W. W. Norton & Company*

9. *Bruce Lee (2015). "Bruce Lee Jeet Kune Do: Bruce Lee's Commentaries on the Martial Way", p.376, Tuttle Publishing*

10. Fromm, Erich. *To have or to be?* Edited by Ruth Nanda Anshen, Harper & Row, 1976. p.24

11. Fromm, Erich. *Man for Himself: An Inquiry Into the Psychology of Ethics*. Henry Holt and Company, 1990. p.84

12. Fromm, Erich. *Man for Himself: An Inquiry Into the Psychology of Ethics*. Henry Holt and Company, 1990. P.45

13. Damasio, Antonio R. *The Feeling of what Happens: Body and Emotion in the Making of Consciousness*. Harcourt Brace, 1999. P. 168-169

14. "Losing Paradise." *YouTube*, 29 October 2012, https://www.youtube.com/watch?v=fWTd-jwUOjU&ab_channel=SimonBrighton.

15. Stanley, Colin, and Colin Wilson. *Super Consciousness: The Quest for the Peak Experience*. Watkins Media, 2019. p.90

16. "Losing Paradise." *YouTube*, 29 October 2012, https://www.youtube.com/watch?v=fWTd-jwUOjU&ab_channel=SimonBrighton 58:52

17. Pieper, Josef. *Leisure: The Basis of Culture ; The Philosophical Act*. p.19

18. Pieper, Josef. *Leisure: The Basis of Culture ; The Philosophical Act*. Ignatius Press, 2009. P.105

19. "Losing Paradise." *YouTube*, 29 October 2012, 53:51 https://www.youtube.com/watch?v=fWTd-jwUOjU&ab_channel=SimonBrighton.

20. Csikszentmihalyi, Mihaly. *Flow: The Psychology of Optimal Experience*. HarperCollins, 2008. p.68

21. *Ralph Waldo Emerson (1983). "Essays and Lectures", p.478, Library of America*

22. *Gwendolyn Brooks (2005). "The Essential Gwendolyn Brooks", p.129, Library of America*

23. "The Art of Stress-Free Productivity: David Allen at TEDxClaremontColleges." *YouTube*, 31 October 2012, https://www.youtube.com/watch?v=CHxhjDPKfbY&ab_channel=TEDxTalks

24. Fromm, Erich. *Man for Himself: An Inquiry Into the Psychology of Ethics*. Henry Holt and Company, 1990. p.10

25. Einstein, Albert. "Albert Einstein, Course Author | AMNH." *American Museum of Natural History*, https://www.amnh.org/learn-teach/seminars-on-science/about/faculty/albert-einstein.

26. Vitale, Tom. "Billie Holiday: Emotional Power Through Song." *NPR*, 22 November 2010, https://www.npr.org/2010/11/19/131451449/billie-holiday-emotional-power-through-song.

27. Stanley, Colin, and Colin Wilson. *Super Consciousness: The Quest for the Peak Experience*. Watkins Media, 2019.p.85

28. James, William. *The Varieties of Religious Experience*. Random House Publishing Group, 1999. p.219

29. Young, Arthur M. *The Reflexive Universe: Evolution of Consciousness*. Anodos Foundation, 1999. p.xxiii-xxiv

30. Eicher, David. "Ask Astro: How quickly is the Moon moving away from Earth?" *Astronomy Magazine*, 23 August 2022, https://astronomy.com/magazine/ask-astro/2022/08/ask-astro-how-quickly-is-the-moon-moving-away-from-earth. Accessed 16 November 2022.

31. Spinoza, Benedictus de. *The Ethics and Selected Letters*. p.15

32. "Heart rate variability: How it might indicate well-being." *Harvard Health*, 22 November 2017, https://www.health.harvard.edu/blog/heart-rate-variability-new-way-track-well-2017112212789.

33. Title:Grey Fahy on the TRIIM-X Trial at EARD2021

34. Young, Arthur M. *The Reflexive Universe: Evolution of Consciousness*. Anodos Foundation, 1999. p.11

35. Teilhard de Chardin, Pierre. *The Phenomenon of Man*. HarperCollins, 2008. p.27

36. Stanley, Colin, and Colin Wilson. *Super Consciousness: The Quest for the Peak Experience*. Watkins Media, 2019. p.80

37. Wilson, Colin. *The Age of Defeat*. Edited by Samantha Devin, Aristeia Press, 2018. p.118

38. Schelling, FWJ. *System des trancendentalen Idealismus*. Gesammelte Schriften, 1794-1800.

39. *"Choruses from the Rock" pt. 1 (1934)*

40. Teilhard de Chardin, Pierre. *The Phenomenon of Man*. HarperCollins, 2008. po.31

41. Whitman, Walt (1892). Essay in *November. Prose Works*. Philadelphia: David McKay

42. *"The Lowest Animal" (1940)*

43. Bachelard, Gaston. *The Poetics of Space*. Translated by Maria Jolas, Penguin Publishing Group, 2014. P. 202

44. Young, Arthur M. *The Reflexive Universe: Evolution of Consciousness*. Anodos Foundation, 1999. p.xix

45. Wilson, Colin. *The Outsider*. Pan Books, 1978. p.30

46. Wilson, Colin. *The Outsider*. Pan Books, 1978 p.39

47. Young, Arthur M. *The Reflexive Universe: Evolution of Consciousness*. Anodos Foundation, 1999. Pp. 48-51

48. Maslow, Abraham H. *Toward a psychology of being*. Wiley, 1999.p.67-69

Printed in Great Britain
by Amazon

33478507R00076